More Daley Bread

HEARTY WHOLEMEAL AND SPECIAL DIET LOAVES IN YOUR BREAD MACHINE

BY GEORGE DALE

PENGUIN BOOKS

PENGUIN BOOKS
Penguin Books (NZ) Ltd, cnr Airborne and Rosedale Roads,
Albany, Auckland 1310, New Zealand
Penguin Books Ltd, 27 Wrights Lane, London W8 5TZ, England
Penguin Putnam Inc, 375 Hudson Street, New York, NY 10014,
United States
Penguin Books Australia Ltd, 487 Maroondah Highway, Ringwood,
Australia 3134
Penguin Books Canada Ltd, 10 Alcorn Avenue, Toronto, Ontario,
Canada M4V 3B2
Penguin Books (South Africa) Pty Ltd, 4 Pallinghurst Road, Parktown,
Johannesburg 2193, South Africa
Penguin Books India (P) Ltd, 11, Community Centre, Panchsheel Park,
New Delhi 110 017, India

Penguin Books Ltd, Registered Offices:
Harmondsworth, Middlesex, England

This edition first published by Penguin Books (NZ) Ltd, 1999
Originally published by GP Publications 1997

1 2 3 4 5 6 7 8 9 10

Designed by Artrage, Wellington

Printed in Australia by Australian Print Group, Maryborough

acknowledgements

Without the stimulus provided by the encouragement and assistance of many people, this book would still be just a couple of files of notes on my desk.

Thank you everybody, especially:

My family, principally my wife, Joy, whose stoicism in the face of extreme bread manifestation is truly amazing.

My publishers, editors, and staff for their faith in the project.

Angela Hallam, whose skill in introducing my dictated and written word to the silicon dream machine is awesome indeed.

Kathie Hope, whose expert culinary knowledge tested many of my recipes and so helped me to perfect them.

To all my friends and colleagues, whose arduous task it was to sample test loaves, generally at morning tea time!

Once again, thanks.

'A little of
what you fancy
does you good.'

Marie Lloyd
1870-1922

contents

page

contents continued

page

introduction

This book, like its predecessor *Daley Bread*, will help you exploit the unique capability of your breadmaker – to make a perfectly baked loaf of your choice at the moment you want it. No fuss, no effort or waste.

Here are 75 recipes gleaned over many years from many sources – chefs, cooks, bakers, my Gran, other breadmaker users, and the many folk who have shared their family recipe books with me. All tried and tested (after being adapted) to suit your breadmaker.

The recipes are grouped so that you may turn directly to those that make the kind of bread that interests you the most.

All raw materials are discussed fully in the ingredients section, with items of special interest being mentioned as required in the recipe or group notes.

All the recipes are user friendly. They use volume measures in international metric cups and spoons, and ingredients that are available in most supermarkets and health food shops.

The tables of measures have been expanded to include amounts for the larger capacity machines now available, although the favourite is still the 1½lb/750g size. See Table 1 to make adjustments of loaf sizes to suit your breadmaker.

Read the recipes from the top, the prompts are arranged in order most likely to assist.

Do take a little time to re-read the Operating Instructions that were supplied with your machine. A thorough understanding of your machine capacities is the key to success, especially with some of the more dense loaf recipes in this book.

If you have troubles, turn to ABOUT UNEXPECTED RESULTS for a solution to your problem.

If you still have troubles – turn to HELP! at the end of this book. This unique service is available only from Daley Bread.

Bon appetit!

I recommend you remove the new loaf as soon as it is baked. Let it cool on a wire rack to get the best result.

Most modern breadmakers have three settings or modes in 'Basic Bake'. These are used for most of the recipes in this book. Other breadmaker settings are generally referred to as 'French Bread', 'Sweet Bread' and 'Fruit Bread'. All these involve a longer cycle because they need longer rise periods. Most breadmakers also have one or two 'Whole Wheat Bread' or 'Multigrain' settings which need longer time. At least one of the older machines has just one programme, called 'Bread', with no variations!

Refer to the instruction book that came with your breadmaker. It will tell you exactly how the cycles work. Some more recent models also have special cycles for making dough or for cooking rice, pasta or jam. However, the recipes in this book only deal with producing yeast risen bread.

- Whatever breadmaker you have, a quick study of the instruction book that came with it, in conjunction with the instructions and recipes in this book, will only add to the success of your baking efforts.

Capacities

Each machine has a nominal capacity or normal loaf size. This is usually rated at about 500 grams (1 lb in older models) for a finished loaf, rising through about 750 grams (1½ lb) which is usual for most machines in use today, and up to 1 kilogram (2 lb) or larger for some of the more recent machines.

To find out the normal loaf size of your breadmaker, refer to the recipe for the basic white bread loaf that came with your machine and see how many cups of flour are used. (Should your recipe give the amount of flour needed in grams then a simple division of this amount by 150 grams will give you an answer in cups.) I classify a breadmaker that calls for up to two cups of flour as a 500 gram (1 lb) machine, up to 3 cups of flour as a 750 gram (1½ lb) machine and up to 4 cups of flour as a 1 kilogram (2 lb) machine.

You will see that all the recipes in this book are laid out for breadmakers of 500g/1 lb, 750g/1½ lb or 1kg/2 lb. All you do is to select the weight list that applies to your breadmaker. Note that you can successfully make a loaf smaller than your machine's normal loaf size, but the crust will probably be firmer.

Adding Ingredients

Most breadmakers have a signal, generally a 'beep', to tell you when to add special ingredients. This is because some ingredients, like fruit or nuts, could get severely damaged in the initial mixing and kneading processes. This signal usually happens near the end of the final kneading.

In this book, special ingredients are listed separately, at the end of the recipe. Should your machine not be able to signal 'add ingredients', add them during the last ten minutes of the final kneading.

Crusts

Some machines have a crust colour selector. Some alter the length of the baking period some adjust the baking temperature. Be careful when using this selector at its lower or lighter level because in some recipes that could result in the middle of the loaf not being fully cooked.

- When using a recipe you haven't tried before, set the crust control in the middle. Depending on how your first loaf turned out, you can then adjust the control up or down for your next loaves.

Bread Pans and Kneading Blades

- Take the bread pan out of the breadmaker before you place the ingredients in the pan.

  If anything is spilled, it will be on the bench top, not in the breadmaker oven. But watch out! This is not an option if the bread pan is the type with a hole in the bottom for the kneading blade.

- Always clean the bread pan as soon as it is cool enough to handle. If the kneading blade has come off the shaft with the loaf, make sure that you recover it from the said loaf, clean it and return it to the shaft. If the kneading blade has stayed on the shaft after you have removed a loaf, put some water in the pan to soak the blade before cleaning.

- It is essential that the kneading blade is removed every time the pan is cleaned - a build up of old bread deposits under the blade can sometimes have quite an unsavoury effect on your next new loaf!

Cleaning

The bread pan and kneading blade (kneader) have specially coated surfaces. Treat them gently:

- Soak off any bread residue with warm water.
- Wash with warm, soapy water and a soft washing up brush.
- Don't scrape or scratch. Don't scour with pads, pastes, powders or liquids.
- Never wash pan or blade in the dishwasher.
- Rinse detergent off thoroughly as it can inhibit the yeast in your next loaf.
- Clean the rest of the breadmaker with a soft cloth wrung out in warm, soapy water.

Delayed Starter Times

All breadmakers are equipped with delayed start timers that allow you to delay the finishing time of your loaf for up to 13 hours. The timer allows you to set the breadmaker overnight so that you have fresh bread for breakfast, or to set it during the day so that you come home to fresh bread in the evening. However not all breads can be cooked from a delayed start because some include ingredients that can deteriorate during the delay.

- All of the recipes in this book have notes attached to let you know whether they are suitable for delayed start or not.

Instruction Books

Take a little time to study all the literature that comes with your breadmaker. Some recipes might be beyond its capabilities, but the instructions will tell you where the limits are.

Maintenance

After each use, when your breadmaker has cooled:

- unplug the power cord
- remove crumbs, flour and any other debris from the oven cavity with a soft, damp cloth
- wipe the outside and lid with a soft, damp cloth
- do not immerse any part of the breadmaker in water, or put water in the oven cavity
- do not use any cleaner, solid or liquid
- do not lubricate any parts.

After some use, the oven cavity and bread pan will develop a patina. This is quite normal.

Service

- The most likely need for service will be replacement of the kneading shaft assembly in the bread pan.
- Have the machine checked by a service agent if any part is damaged or malfunctioning. Always get an estimate first for any repair.
- Contact your breadmaker retailer for replacement parts.
- See HELP! at the end of this book.

about the ingredients and recipes

Bread is only as good as what goes into it. Use ingredients as fresh as you can get and always check the use by dates.

All the ingredients listed in the recipes can be found in most supermarkets and health food stores. If you have troubles see HELP! at the end of this book.

Flours

High Grade flour or 'bread' flour is the basic white flour used in most recipes because of its high level of gluten-forming protein.

Wholemeal flour is similar to white refined flour, but some germ and bran is put back into it after refining.

Stoneground Wholemeal flour is the complete milled grain with the germ and bran left in. Wholemeal flours and those made from other cereals - oats, rice, rye, corn or barley - form much less gluten so that breads containing these flours are denser and have a crumbly texture. Gluten flour is added to some recipes to compensate for the lack of proteins in the other ingredients.

- *Never use self-raising flours (see UNEXPECTED RESULTS).*
- *Store FLOUR in the original bag placed in an airtight container. (Wholemeal flour is best kept in the fridge - especially stoneground flour.)*

Gluten Flour

Use with wholemeal and other low-protein flours to boost the gluten structure. Add at the rate of ½ to 1 tablespoon per cup of wholemeal flour or 1 tablespoon per cup of other cereal flours.

- *Check liquidity when using gluten (more may be required).*
- *Store in an airtight container in the fridge.*

Vital Wheat Gluten

Use as Gluten Flour (above), but reduce measures to **teaspoons** instead of tablespoons.

- *Store in an airtight container in the fridge.*

Wheat Germ

Use in some recipes to add nutrients. Can go rancid if stored too long, as can the bread containing it.

- *Store in an airtight container in the fridge.*

Bran

Use to add fibre. Bran is removed from the grain during milling.

- *Recipes with bran may need extra liquid.*

Cracked Wheat

Coarsely ground whole wheat; use it to add texture.

- *Store in an airtight container.*

Bread Mixes

Prepacked bread mixes are obtainable at most supermarkets. The usual selection is white, wholemeal or multigrain. The basic mix requires only the addition of water and yeast. Some breadmaker instruction books have recipes that use mixes. I don't use them myself as I find the size of the bags of pre-mixed ingredients too large. This restricts my choice of bread to that mix, until the bag is used up.

- *Store in original bag in an airtight container.*

Yeasts

Most of the recipes in the book use Surebake yeast. However, for gluten free and wheat free recipes, use active dried yeast instead because the 'improvers' in Surebake are not compatible with these recipes.

- *Beware of 'Instant Dried Yeast' as the results can be dramatic, to say the least (see UNEXPECTED RESULTS).*
- *Never dissolve the yeast in water; just put it in dry.*
- *Only use ingredients at room temperature as heat kills yeast and cold slows the action.*
- *Store in the jar in the fridge. Check the use by date.*

Sugar

Sugar sweetens the bread and aids browning. It also supplies carbohydrates for fermentation to 'feed' the yeast.

- *Use any form of sugar you like - white, brown, honey, treacle, molasses or golden syrup.*
- *Never use artificial sweeteners.*
- *When replacing solid sugars with liquid reduce the liquid quantity in the recipe to compensate.*

Salt

Use ordinary table salt or sea salt. Salt contributes to an even textured bread and helps keep the carbon dioxide under control during fermentation.

- *Never use salt replacements as they just do not work here.*
- *Be careful with the quantities of yeast, sugar and salt. Together they delicately*

balance to form gluten, start fermentation and produce carbon dioxide. Adjustment of any by quite small amounts will considerably affect the volume and texture of the finished product. (See UNEXPECTED RESULTS.)

- *Beware of a salt content in other ingredients and reduce salt ingredient to compensate.*

Fats

Choose any you like: butter, shortening, lecithin granules, olive oil, seed or vegetable oils or margarine. Fats add flavour and robustness to the bread. They also help bread to keep better.

- *If replacing lecithin granules with liquid lecithin, reduce recipe amount by half.*
- *When replacing solid fats with oil, reduce the liquid quantity in the recipe to compensate.*

Liquids

Water, juices, yoghurt, soy milk or cow's milk are called for in the recipes. If you use whole fresh milk instead of milk powder you will need to adjust the amount of fats and liquid to compensate for the extra fats and liquid in the milk.

- *A lot of recipes make a big issue of the temperature of the ingredients, especially the liquids. I recommend 18°-20° C (room temperature) for everything. In all the testing I have done, in a great variety of breadmakers, the temperature was never a problem.*
- *Never use fresh milk or juices with a delayed start (timer) programme because those ingredients might spoil while waiting.*

Eggs

I only ever use whole eggs (never separated). If the recipe calls for eggs without specifying size, use what eggs you have to hand, beat the white and yolk together, place in your liquid measure and add other liquid ingredient(s) up to the total liquid level required.

- *Never use egg with a delayed start (timer) programme as the egg might spoil while waiting.*
- *I usually allow 3 tablespoons when calculating the amount of liquid per egg in a recipe.*

Fruits

Usually dried, sometimes fresh can be used. If using fresh don't forget to adjust the sugar and liquid amounts slightly to allow for the content of the fruit.

Nuts

Any type of nuts can be substituted for those stated in the recipes.

- *Always chop nuts, not too coarsely.*

Herbs and Spices

All the herbs and spices used in the recipes in this book are of the dried, ready prepared variety that you can purchase from any supermarket. Substitute fresh herbs by all means, but remember that dried herbs are more potent than fresh ones. Therefore if you use fresh herbs at least double the quantity.

- *The small airtight containers of dried herbs and spices should be stored in a cool, dark cupboard away from light and heat.*

Dried Milk

The recipes in this book use dried whole milk. You may substitute any other dried milk powder but you may need to adjust fat content to compensate.

Cheese

Most cheeses can be substituted in the recipes for other similar textured cheese.

- *Always check - if a cheese is 'extra' salty reduce the salt in the recipe.*
- *Make sure soft cheeses such as feta or cottage are well drained before use.*

Essences and Flavourings

If liquid, measure and include with the main liquid in the recipe.

- *If flavouring with soy, or other sauces such as Worcester, reduce the salt in the recipe.*

about using and maintaining your breadmaker

No matter what size or shape your breadmaker, it will make bread quickly and easily. All you do is place the ingredients in the bread pan, select the programme, and press the right buttons. The machine does all the work. Oh, you have to remove the bread and eat it, of course.

Some breadmakers just appear to do nothing at first, but they are assessing and adjusting the temperature of the ingredients. This can take up to 45 minutes.

Most breadmakers go through this sequence:

- first mix, or knead
- first rise
- punch down or second mix (to release gas)
- second rise
- shaping
- final rise
- baking
- cooling.

Measuring

It is essential that all ingredients are measured accurately. All the recipes and tables of quantities in this book use the standard international metric volume measures, in cups, tablespoons and teaspoons.

- *Beware the ubiquitous Australian tablespoon! It is 5ml larger than the international metric standard.*

Scoop up the ingredients into your cup or spoon; don't pack them into the measure or tap the bottom to settle them. Rather let them fill the measure in a natural fashion without any pressure to get more in. This will produce a more accurate, consistent result. Correct interpretation of all the recipes is most essential because breadmakers are designed to operate strictly within the fixed programmed cycle that you select. The machine operation doesn't vary. Time after time it performs exactly the same actions, governed only by the programme cycle started and stopping automatically, or by you pushing the 'stop' button. The breadmaker, unlike the baker doing the job by hand, cannot adjust to differing quantities of ingredients with a longer kneading or rising time, by leaving the loaf in the oven longer. The machine only does what it is programmed to do, with what you give it to work with.

Because the recipes in this book have been converted for use in different capacity machines, it has resulted in some measurements appearing to be odd, for example measuring $^{2}/_{3}$ of a tablespoon or $^{3}/_{8}$ of a cup. The following chart will help with some of the equivalent measures. For more detailed measures please refer to the Tables at the end of this book.

Equal Measures for Part Cups and Spoons

1	Cup	=	16	Tablespoons	=	48	Teaspoons
7/8	Cup	=	14	Tablespoons	=	42	Teaspoons
	Cup	=	12	Tablespoons	=	36	Teaspoons
5/8	Cup	=	10	Tablespoons	=	30	Teaspoons
½	Cup	=	8	Tablespoons	=	24	Teaspoons
3/8	Cup	=	6	Tablespoons	=	18	Teaspoons
¼	Cup	=	4	Tablespoons	=	12	Teaspoons
1/8	Cup	=	2	Tablespoons	=	6	Teaspoons
			1	Tablespoon	=	3	Teaspoons
				Tablespoon	=	2¼	Teaspoons
			2/3	Tablespoon	=	2	Teaspoons
			½	Tablespoon	=	1½	Teaspoons
			1/3	Tablespoon	=	1	Teaspoon
			¼	Tablespoon	=		Teaspoon

- Your cup measure should be 250ml capacity and graduated in 1/8 cup steps.
- Your spoon set should contain:

1	15ml	Tablespoon
1	5ml	Teaspoon
1	2.5ml	½ Teaspoon
1	1.25ml	¼ Teaspoon

Other points to note are:

- *Some older or low power machines may not cope with recipes with a lot of heavy grains.*
- *To adjust the recipes to suit the new extra large capacity breadmakers refer to Table 5.*

Order of Ingredients

You must place the ingredients in the pan in the order laid down in the instruction book that came with your breadmaker.

The recipes in this book are all listed with the dry items first, liquid items last. Your breadmaker's instruction book might ask you to do it the other way around. If so, just start at the bottom of the recipes in this book and work through to the top!

Some might think it doesn't matter which order you use, but believe me it does, especially when using a delayed start.

Programmes

Use the programme cycles recommended for the recipes in this book. Your breadmaker might call them something different. Look in its recipe book for a recipe using similar ingredients, in similar quantities, and use the programme that it suggests. See also notes on programme cycles in ABOUT USING AND MAINTAINING YOUR BREADMAKER.

Delayed Start

Use only the recipes recommended as suitable for the delayed start programmes as the other recipes contain ingredients that might spoil during the waiting period.

Whole Grains

When using kibbled or whole grains in a recipe, measure out the exact amount of water to be used in the recipe and bring it to the boil. Put the amount of grains required in the recipe in a bowl. Pour the boiling water onto the grains and let them soak for 10-20 minutes. Finally, strain the grains, reserving any water that is left. Allow the grains to cool, then add them to the dry ingredients. The reserved water should be measured with other liquids in the recipe.

Measuring Sticky Ingredients

Treat the measuring cup or spoon with oil first. The 'sticky stuff' - honey, molasses or peanut butter - will then slide off quite easily.

Liquidity Check

Because the moisture content of flour and other ingredients varies all the time, mainly due to environmental conditions, you should check the mixture after the first five minutes of mixing or kneading. The dough should have a smooth 'satin' look and be slightly sticky.

If it is too sticky or wet looking, add flour one tablespoon at a time. If the dough looks stiff and 'tight', add water one tablespoon at a time.

Use a rubber spatula (see HELP! at the end of this book) to scrape down ingredients adhering to the pot sides during mixing or kneading.

Storing Your Loaves

This aspect of bread making is not usually a problem for most breadmaker users. When it is no chore to have fresh made bread on demand, why bother to store? On the other hand, many people living alone find half a loaf or less is all they need each day so it makes good sense to cut the fresh loaf in two - use half and store half.

I recommend that you cool the loaf on a wire rack, wrap it tightly in foil, then seal it in a plastic bag before freezing. Most breads from recipes in this book will still be good after several weeks in the freezer. When you remove the loaf from the freezer, keep it in the plastic bag, allow it to thaw naturally - not in the microwave! - remove the plastic bag, put the loaf (still foil wrapped) in the oven for 20-30 minutes at 170ºC. Open the foil for the last 5 minutes. Delicious.

Basic breads

one

Beginners please! Here are three easy breads to start you off. They will please experts as well as beginners.

George's basic test loaf

Looks good, tastes good, and economical too.

Ingredients	**Measure**	500g (1 lb)	750g (1½ lb)	1kg (2 lb)
Surebake Yeast	Teaspoon	2	3	4
High Grade Flour	Cup	2	3	4
Sugar	Tablespoon	¾	1	1½
Salt	Teaspoon	¾	1	1½
Water	Cup	¾	1⅛	1½

- Check the 'normal loaf size' for your bread machine in the USING YOUR BREADMAKER section.
- This recipe can be used with Time Delay.
- Place ingredients in the bread pan in the order recommended in your machine instruction book.
- Fit pan in machine, select Basic Bake cycle and press Start.
- Check liquidity of ingredients.
- Remove bread from pan at end of Bake and place on a rack to cool.

Good English bread

Thin for sandwiches, thick for toast.

Ingredients	Measure	500g (1 lb)	750g (1½ lb)	1kg (2 lb)
Surebake Yeast	Teaspoon	2	3	4
High Grade Flour	Cup	2	3	4
Sugar	Tablespoon	½	¾	1
Salt	Teaspoon	½	¾	1
Shortening	Tablespoon	1	1½	2
Egg (measure with water)		1	1	2
Water	Cup	¾	1⅛	1½

- Check the 'normal loaf size' for your bread machine in the USING YOUR BREADMAKER section.
- Do not use Time Delay with this recipe.
- Place ingredients in the bread pan in the order recommended in your machine instruction book.
- Fit pan in machine, select Basic Bake cycle and press Start.
- Check liquidity of ingredients.
- Sprinkle on some poppy seeds just before Bake.
- Remove bread from pan at end of Bake and place on a rack to cool.

Plain wholemeal bread

A good base for your favourite sandwich.

Ingredients	Measure	500g (1 lb)	750g (1½ lb)	1kg (2 lb)
Surebake Yeast	Teaspoon	2	3	4
Wholemeal Flour	Cup	2	3	4
Gluten Flour	Tablespoon	2	3	4
Salt	Teaspoon	½	¾	1
Lecithin	Tablespoon	⅔	1	1⅓
Milk Powder	Tablespoon	1⅓	2	2⅔
Honey	Tablespoon	1⅓	2	2⅔
Water	Cup	¾	1⅛	1½

- Check the 'normal loaf size' for your bread machine in the USING YOUR BREADMAKER section.
- This recipe can be used with Time Delay.
- Place ingredients in the bread pan in the order recommended in your machine instruction book.
- Fit pan in machine, select Wholemeal Bake cycle and press Start.
- Check liquidity of ingredients.
- Remove bread from pan at end of Bake and place on a rack to cool.

White speciality and white breads

two

The loaves in this section are all made with delicious, perhaps unusual ingredients, and high grade white flour. I like these recipes - they are not at all hedonistic, well, most of them are not. Included here are several recipes from my first book because a lot of people liked them, plus some new ones.

Avocado, cheese and herb bread

My favourite colour - green!

Ingredients	**Measure**	500g (1 lb)	750g (1½ lb)	1kg (2 lb)
Surebake Yeast	Teaspoon	2	3	4
High Grade Flour	Cup	2	3	4
Sugar	Tablespoon	½	¾	1
Salt	Teaspoon	½	¾	1
Avocado (mashed with 1 tspn lemon juice)	Cup	½	¾	1
Grated Tasty Cheese	Cup	½	¾	1
Dried Parsley	Teaspoon	1	1½	2
Dried Thyme	Teaspoon	1	1½	2
Dried Basil	Teaspoon	1	1½	2
Water	Cup	5/8	1	1¼

- Check the 'normal loaf size' for your bread machine in the USING YOUR BREADMAKER section.
- Do not use Time Delay with this recipe.
- Place ingredients in the bread pan in the order recommended in your machine instruction book.
- Fit pan in machine, select Basic Bake cycle and press Start.
- Check liquidity of ingredients.
- Brush top of loaf with milk and sprinkle with pumpkin seed before Bake.
- Remove bread from pan at end of Bake and place on a rack to cool.

Semolina French Bread

Fresh for breakfast - c'est magnifique.

Ingredients	**Measure**	500g (1 lb)	750g (1½ lb)	1kg (2 lb)
Surebake Yeast	Teaspoon	2	3	4
High Grade Flour	Cup	1	1½	2
Semolina Flour	Cup	1	1½	2
Sugar	Tablespoon	½	1	1½
Salt	Teaspoon	¼	½	¾
Water	Cup	¾	1⅛	1½

- Check the 'normal loaf size' for your bread machine in the USING YOUR BREADMAKER section.
- This recipe can be used with Time Delay.
- Place ingredients in the bread pan in the order recommended in your machine instruction book.
- Fit pan in machine, select Basic Bake cycle and press Start.
- Check liquidity of ingredients.
- Remove bread from pan at end of Bake and place on a rack to cool.

Cornmeal and honey loaf

Slightly crunchy.

Ingredients	Measure	500g (1 lb)	750g (1½ lb)	1kg (2 lb)
Surebake Yeast	Teaspoon	2	3	4
High Grade Flour	Cup	1½	2¼	3
Cornmeal	Cup	½	¾	1
Lecithin	Tablespoon	1	1½	2
Milk Powder	Tablespoon	1⅓	2	2⅔
Honey	Tablespoon	1⅓	2	2⅔
Salt	Teaspoon	½	¾	1
Water	Cup	¾	1⅛	1½

- Check the 'normal loaf size' for your bread machine in the USING YOUR BREADMAKER section.
- This recipe can be used with Time Delay.
- Place ingredients in the bread pan in the order recommended in your machine instruction book.
- Fit pan in machine, select Basic Bake cycle and press Start.
- Check liquidity of ingredients.
- Remove bread from pan at end of Bake and place on a rack to cool.

George's rum baba

Named after Ali - beware the forty thieves when you make this. Spoon rum syrup over as you serve the portions.

Ingredients	Measure	500g (1 lb)	750g (1½ lb)	1kg (2 lb)
Surebake Yeast	Teaspoon	2	3	4
High Grade Flour	Cup	2	3	4
Sugar	Tablespoon	2	3	4
Salt	Teaspoon	1	1½	2
Milk Powder	Tablespoon	1	1½	2
Lecithin	Tablespoon	2	3	4
Almond Extract	Teaspoon	½	¾	1
Vanilla Extract	Teaspoon	½	¾	1
Egg (measure with water)		1	2	3
Water	Cup	¾	1⅛	1½
Raisins	Cup	½	¾	1
Slivered Almonds	Cup	¼	½	¾

- Check the 'normal loaf size' for your bread machine in the USING YOUR BREADMAKER section.
- Do not use Time Delay with this recipe.
- Place first ten ingredients in the bread pan in the order recommended in your machine instruction book.
- Fit pan in machine, select Basic Bake cycle and press Start.
- Check liquidity of ingredients.
- Place remaining ingredients in pan when 'beep' sounds, or ten minutes from end of final kneading.
- Remove bread from pan at end of Bake and place on a rack to cool.

Yoghurt and honey loaf

Hedonistic and healthy!

Ingredients	**Measure**	500g (1 lb)	750g (1½ lb)	1kg (2 lb)
Surebake Yeast	Teaspoon	2	3	4
High Grade Flour	Cup	2	3	4
Honey	Tablespoon	1	1½	2
Salt	Teaspoon	½	¾	1
Plain Yoghurt	Cup	¾	1⅛	1½

- Check the 'normal loaf size' for your bread machine in the USING YOUR BREADMAKER section.
- Do not use Time Delay with this recipe.
- Place ingredients in the bread pan in the order recommended in your machine instruction book.
- Fit pan in machine, select Basic Bake cycle and press Start.
- Check liquidity of ingredients.
- Remove bread from pan at end of Bake and place on a rack to cool.

Kumara, apple and sultana bread

Kumara with apple? Try it!!

Ingredients	**Measure**	500g (1 lb)	750g (1½ lb)	1kg (2 lb)
Surebake Yeast	Teaspoon	2	3	4
High Grade Flour	Cup	2	3	4
Sugar	Tablespoon	1⅓	2	2⅔
Salt	Teaspoon	½	¾	1
Kumara (cooked, drained and mashed)	Cup	⅝	1	1¼
Lecithin	Tablespoon	1	1½	2
Lemon Juice	Teaspoon	1	1½	2
Milk Powder	Tablespoon	1⅓	2	2⅔
Water	Cup	¾	1⅛	1½
Chopped Dried Apple	Cup	½	¾	1
Sultanas	Cup	⅜	½	¾

- Check the 'normal loaf size' for your bread machine in the USING YOUR BREADMAKER section.
- Do not use Time Delay with this recipe.
- Place first nine ingredients in the bread pan in the order recommended in your machine instruction book.
- Fit pan in machine, select Basic Bake Raisin cycle and press Start.
- Check liquidity of ingredients.
- Place remaining ingredients in pan when 'beep' sounds, or ten minutes from end of final kneading.
- Remove bread from pan at end of Bake and place on a rack to cool.

Potato and sesame bread

Make your bacon sandwiches with this one.

Ingredients	**Measure**	500g (1 lb)	750g (1½ lb)	1kg (2 lb)
Surebake Yeast	Teaspoon	2	3	4
High Grade Flour	Cup	2	3	4
Instant Mashed Potato Flakes	Tablespoon	2¾	4	5½
Milk Powder	Tablespoon	1	1½	2
Sugar	Tablespoon	1	1½	2
Salt	Teaspoon	½	¾	1
Lecithin	Tablespoon	1½	2¼	3
Egg (measure with water)		1	1	2
Sesame Seeds	Tablespoon	1	1½	2
Parsley	Teaspoon	1	1½	2
Water	Cup	7/8	1 3/8	1¾

- Check the 'normal loaf size' for your bread machine in the USING YOUR BREADMAKER section.
- Do not use Time Delay with this recipe.
- Place ingredients in the bread pan in the order recommended in your machine instruction book.
- Fit pan in machine, select Basic Bake cycle and press Start.
- Check liquidity of ingredients.
- Remove bread from pan at end of Bake and place on a rack to cool.

Rosie's herb bread

Adapted from a handmade original.

Ingredients	Measure	500g (1 lb)	750g (1½ lb)	1kg (2 lb)
Surebake Yeast	Teaspoon	2	3	4
High Grade Flour	Cup	2	3	4
Milk Powder	Tablespoon	1	1½	2
Lecithin	Tablespoon	1	1½	2
Sugar	Tablespoon	⅔	1	1⅓
Salt	Teaspoon	½	¾	1
Thyme	Teaspoon	½	¾	1
Sage	Teaspoon	½	¾	1
Basil	Teaspoon	½	¾	1
Water	Cup	¾	1⅛	1½

- Check the 'normal loaf size' for your bread machine in the USING YOUR BREADMAKER section.
- This recipe can be used with Time Delay.
- Place ingredients in the bread pan in the order recommended in your machine instruction book.
- Fit pan in machine, select Basic Bake cycle and press Start.
- Check liquidity of ingredients.
- Remove bread from pan at end of Bake and place on a rack to cool.

Cinnamon chocolate - drop loaf

Only slightly decadent.

Ingredients	**Measure**	500g (1 lb)	750g (1½ lb)	1kg (2 lb)
Surebake Yeast	Teaspoon	2	3	4
High Grade Flour	Cup	2	3	4
Brown Sugar	Tablespoon	2	3	4
Salt	Teaspoon	½	¾	1
Milk Powder	Tablespoon	1	1½	2
Lecithin	Tablespoon	1	1½	2
Cinnamon	Teaspoon	½	1	1½
Water	Cup	¾	1⅛	1½
Dark Chocolate Drops (Frozen)	Cup	¼	½	¾

- Check the 'normal loaf size' for your bread machine in the USING YOUR BREADMAKER section.
- Do not use Time Delay with this recipe.
- Place first eight ingredients in the bread pan in the order recommended in your machine instruction book.
- Fit pan in machine, select Basic Bake Raisin and press Start.
- Check liquidity of ingredients.
- Place remaining ingredients in pan when 'beep' sounds, or ten minutes from end of final kneading. (Keep in freezer until just before.)
- Remove bread from pan at end of Bake and place on a rack to cool.

50/50 Wholemeal and other flour breads

three

Some like a good 'strong' wholemeal flavour, but a lot of folk prefer a milder one. Besides, mixing flours makes wholemeal flour a better foil for other more delicate or unusual ingredients.

Bean sprout and pumpkin seed loaf

Nutriment with exciting new flavours.

Ingredients	**Measure**	500g (1 lb)	750g (1½ lb)	1kg (2 lb)
Surebake Yeast	Teaspoon	2	3	4
High Grade Flour	Cup	1	1½	2
Wholemeal Flour	Cup	1	1½	2
Gluten Flour	Tablespoon	1	1½	2
Molasses	Tablespoon	½	¾	1
Salt	Teaspoon	½	¾	1
Milk Powder	Tablespoon	2¾	4	5½
Lecithin	Tablespoon	1	1½	2
Bean Sprouts	Cup	5/8	1	1¼
Pumpkin Seeds	Cup	3/8	½	¾
Water	Cup	7/8	1¼	1¾

- Check the 'normal loaf size' for your bread machine in the USING YOUR BREADMAKER section.
- Do not use Time Delay with this recipe.
- Place ingredients in the bread pan in the order recommended in your machine instruction book.
- Fit pan in machine, select Basic Bake cycle and press Start.
- Check liquidity of ingredients.
- Remove bread from pan at end of Bake and place on a rack to cool.

Brown bread with molasses

Full of flavour.

Ingredients	Measure	500g (1 lb)	750g (1½ lb)	1kg (2 lb)
Surebake Yeast	Teaspoon	2	3	4
High Grade Flour	Cup	1	1½	2
Wholemeal Flour	Cup	1	1½	2
Gluten Flour	Tablespoon	1	1½	2
Molasses	Tablespoon	1⅓	2	2⅔
Salt	Teaspoon	½	¾	1
Lecithin	Tablespoon	1⅓	2	2⅔
Water	Cup	¾	1⅛	1½

- Check the 'normal loaf size' for your bread machine in the USING YOUR BREADMAKER section.
- This recipe can be used with Time Delay.
- Place ingredients in the bread pan in the order recommended in your machine instruction book.
- Fit pan in machine, select Basic Bake cycle and press Start.
- Check liquidity of ingredients.
- Remove bread from pan at end of Bake and place on a rack to cool.

Feta and herb loaf

Tasty, tasty!

Ingredients	Measure	500g (1 lb)	750g (1½ lb)	1kg (2 lb)
Surebake Yeast	Teaspoon	2	3	4
High Grade Flour	Cup	1	1½	2
Wholemeal Flour	Cup	1	1½	2
Gluten Flour	Tablespoon	1	1½	2
Sugar	Tablespoon	1	1½	2
Salt	Teaspoon	¼	¼	½
Caraway Seed	Teaspoon	1	1½	2
Black Pepper	Teaspoon	¼	¼	½
Feta Cheese (crumbled)	Cup	½	¾	1
Water	Cup	¾	1⅛	1½

- Check the 'normal loaf size' for your bread machine in the USING YOUR BREADMAKER section.
- Do not use Time Delay with this recipe.
- Beware! Some goat and sheep milk cheese can be extra salty. Adjust salt in recipe to suit.
- Place ingredients in the bread pan in the order recommended in your machine instruction book.
- Fit pan in machine, select Basic Bake cycle and press Start.
- Check liquidity of ingredients.
- Remove bread from pan at end of Bake and place on a rack to cool.

George's garlic bread

Try this on your dinner guests.

Ingredients	Measure	500g (1 lb)	750g (1½ lb)	1kg (2 lb)
Surebake Yeast	Teaspoon	2	3	4
High Grade Flour	Cup	1	1½	2
Wholemeal Flour	Cup	1	1½	2
Gluten Flour	Tablespoon	1	1½	2
Sugar	Tablespoon	1¼	2	2½
Salt	Teaspoon	1	1½	2
Minced Garlic	Tablespoon	1¼	2	2½
Lecithin	Tablespoon	1½	2	3
Mixed Herbs	Teaspoon	1	1½	2
Water	Cup	¾	1⅛	1½

- Check the 'normal loaf size' for your bread machine in the USING YOUR BREADMAKER section.
- Do not use Time Delay with this recipe.
- Place ingredients in the bread pan in the order recommended in your machine instruction book.
- Fit pan in machine, select Basic Bake cycle and press Start.
- Check liquidity of ingredients.
- Remove bread from pan at end of Bake and place on a rack to cool.

Grant's request - cheese and onion loaf

One that I use for testing in the workshop - drives 'em crazy!

Ingredients	**Measure**	500g (1 lb)	750g (1½ lb)	1kg (2 lb)
Surebake Yeast	Teaspoon	2	3	4
High Grade Flour	Cup	1	1½	2
Wholemeal Flour	Cup	1	1½	2
Gluten Flour	Tablespoon	1	1½	2
Sugar	Tablespoon	½	¾	1
Salt	Teaspoon	½	¾	1
Water	Cup	¾	1⅛	1½
Tasty Cheese (grated)	Cup	½	¾	1
Chopped Onion	Tablespoon	1½	2¼	3

- Check the 'normal loaf size' for your bread machine in the USING YOUR BREADMAKER section.
- Do not use Time Delay with this recipe.
- Place first seven ingredients in the bread pan in the order recommended in your machine instruction book.
- Fit pan in machine, select Wholemeal Bake cycle and press Start.
- Check liquidity of ingredients.
- Place remaining ingredients in pan when 'beep' sounds, or ten minutes from end of final kneading.
- Remove bread from pan at end of Bake and place on a rack to cool.

Maria Fairburn's three seed & kibble loaf

A Wairarapa winner!

Ingredients	**Measure**	500g (1 lb)	750g (1½ lb)	1kg (2 lb)
Surebake Yeast	Teaspoon	2	3	4
High Grade Flour	Cup	1⅝	2½	3¼
Wholemeal Flour	Cup	⅜	½	¾
Kibbled Wheat	Cup	¼	⅜	½
Linseed	Tablespoon	2	3	4
Pumpkin Seed	Tablespoon	2	3	4
Sunflower Seed	Tablespoon	2	3	4
Sugar	Tablespoon	1	1½	2
Salt	Teaspoon	¼	½	¾
Olive Oil	Tablespoon	1	1½	2
Water	Cup	¾	1⅛	1½

- Check the 'normal loaf size' for your bread machine in the USING YOUR BREADMAKER section.
- Do not use Time Delay with this recipe.
- Place ingredients in the bread pan in the order recommended in your machine instruction book.
- Fit pan in machine, select Wholemeal Bake cycle and press Start.
- Check liquidity of ingredients.
- Remove bread from pan at end of Bake and place on a rack to cool.

Milk and honey loaf

Honey flavour and crunchy with nuts.

Ingredients	Measure	500g (1 lb)	750g (1½ lb)	1kg (2 lb)
Surebake Yeast	Teaspoon	2	3	4
High Grade Flour	Cup	1	1½	2
Wholemeal Flour	Cup	1	1½	2
Gluten Flour	Tablespoon	1	1½	2
Honey	Tablespoon	2¾	4	5½
Salt	Teaspoon	½	¾	1
Milk Powder	Tablespoon	2	3	4
Lecithin	Tablespoon	1	1½	2
Water	Cup	⅞	1¼	1¾
Chopped Nuts	Cup	½	¾	1

- Check the 'normal loaf size' for your bread machine in the USING YOUR BREADMAKER section.
- Do not use Time Delay with this recipe.
- Place first nine ingredients in the bread pan in the order recommended in your machine instruction book.
- Fit pan in machine, select Basic Bake Raisin or Sweet cycle and press Start.
- Check liquidity of ingredients.
- Place remaining ingredients in pan when 'beep' sounds, or ten minutes from end of final kneading.
- Remove bread from pan at end of Bake and place on a rack to cool.

Mint wholemeal loaf

With a hint of mint.

Ingredients	Measure	500g (1 lb)	750g (1½ lb)	1kg (2 lb)
Surebake Yeast	Teaspoon	2	3	4
High Grade Flour	Cup	1	1½	2
Wholemeal Flour	Cup	1	1½	2
Gluten Flour	Tablespoon	1	1½	2
Milk Powder	Tablespoon	1⅓	2	2⅔
Lecithin	Tablespoon	⅔	1	1⅓
Lemon Juice	Teaspoon	1	1½	2
Honey	Tablespoon	⅔	1	1⅓
Chopped Fresh Mint	Tablespoon	2	3	4
Water	Cup	¾	1⅛	1½

- Check the 'normal loaf size' for your bread machine in the USING YOUR BREADMAKER section.
- Do not use Time Delay with this recipe.
- Place ingredients in the bread pan in the order recommended in your machine instruction book.
- Fit pan in machine, select Basic Bake cycle and press Start.
- Check liquidity of ingredients.
- Remove bread from pan at end of Bake and place on a rack to cool.

Wholemeal cottage cheese loaf

Try it toasted also, delicious!

Ingredients	**Measure**	500g (1 lb)	750g (1½ lb)	1kg (2 lb)
Surebake Yeast	Teaspoon	2	3	4
High Grade Flour	Cup	1	1½	2
Wholemeal Flour	Cup	1	1½	2
Gluten Flour	Tablespoon	1	1½	2
Sugar	Tablespoon	1¼	2	2¾
Salt	Teaspoon	¾	1⅛	1½
Butter	Tablespoon	1½	2	2½
Black Pepper	Teaspoon	¾	1⅛	1½
Chopped Onion	Tablespoon	2	3	4
Cottage Cheese	Cup	½	¾	1
Egg (measure with water)		1	1	2
Water	Cup	⅝	1	1¼

- Check the 'normal loaf size' for your bread machine in the USING YOUR BREADMAKER section.
- Do not use Time Delay with this recipe.
- Place ingredients in the bread pan in the order recommended in your machine instruction book.
- Both onion and cheese to be well drained.
- Fit pan in machine, select Basic Bake cycle and press Start.
- Check liquidity of ingredients.
- Remove bread from pan at end of Bake and place on a rack to cool.

100% Wholemeal breads

four

Wheat flour produced from the whole grain - bran, germ, and all, nothing added, nothing taken away - makes a dark flavourful loaf, with more protein than white flour bread.

This dark flour is the perfect partner for many other strong (and spicy) flavours that are teamed with it in the following recipes.

Apple and raisin loaf

Let it cool - if you can!

Ingredients	**Measure**	500g (1 lb)	750g (1½ lb)	1kg (2 lb)
Surebake Yeast	Teaspoon	2	3	4
Wholemeal Flour	Cup	1⅝	2½	3¼
Gluten Flour	Tablespoon	2	3	4
Rolled Oats	Cup	⅜	½	¾
Salt	Teaspoon	½	¾	1
Apple Sauce	Cup	½	¾	1
Water	Cup	¾	1	1¼
Raisins	Cup	⅜	½	¾
Ground Cloves	Teaspoon	¼	½	¾

- Check the 'normal loaf size' for your bread machine in the USING YOUR BREADMAKER section.
- Do not use Time Delay with this recipe.
- Place first seven ingredients in the bread pan in the order recommended in your machine instruction book.
- Fit pan in machine, select Wholemeal Bake Raisin or Sweet cycle and press Start.
- Check liquidity of ingredients.
- Place remaining ingredients in pan when 'beep' sounds, or ten minutes from end of final kneading.
- Remove bread from pan at end of Bake and place on a rack to cool.

Banana and raisin loaf

Eat it warm for afternoon tea.

Ingredients	**Measure**	500g (1 lb)	750g (1½ lb)	1kg (2 lb)
Surebake Yeast	Teaspoon	2	3	4
Wholemeal Flour	Cup	2	3	4
Gluten Flour	Tablespoon	2	3	4
Salt	Teaspoon	½	¾	1
Banana (mashed)	Cup	3/8	½	¾
Water	Cup	¾	1 1/8	1½
Raisins	Cup	3/8	½	¾

- Check the 'normal loaf size' for your bread machine in the USING YOUR BREADMAKER section.
- Do not use Time Delay with this recipe.
- Place first six ingredients in the bread pan in the order recommended in your machine instruction book.
- Fit pan in machine, select Wholemeal Bake Raisin or Sweet cycle and press Start.
- Check liquidity of ingredients.
- Place remaining ingredients in pan when 'beep' sounds, or ten minutes from end of final kneading.
- Remove bread from pan at end of Bake and place on a rack to cool.

Brazilian special

Cafe O.K!

Ingredients	**Measure**	500g (1 lb)	750g (1½ lb)	1kg (2 lb)
Surebake Yeast	Teaspoon	2	3	4
Wholemeal Flour	Cup	2	3	4
Gluten Flour	Tablespoon	2	3	4
Cocoa Powder	Tablespoon	2	3	4
Salt	Teaspoon	½	¾	1
Honey	Tablespoon	1	1½	2
Lecithin	Tablespoon	1⅓	2	2⅔
Coffee (cool, strong brewed)	Cup	¾	1⅛	1½

- Check the 'normal loaf size' for your bread machine in the USING YOUR BREADMAKER section.
- This recipe can be used with Time Delay.
- Place ingredients in the bread pan in the order recommended in your machine instruction book.
- Fit pan in machine, select Basic Bake cycle and press Start.
- Check liquidity of ingredients.
- Remove bread from pan at end of Bake and place on a rack to cool.

Cheese and garlic wholemeal loaf

Try this on your dinner guests!

Ingredients	Measure	500g (1 lb)	750g (1½ lb)	1kg (2 lb)
Surebake Yeast	Teaspoon	2	3	4
Wholemeal Flour	Cup	2	3	4
Gluten Flour	Tablespoon	2	3	4
Honey	Tablespoon	1⅓	2	2⅔
Salt	Teaspoon	½	¾	1
Minced Garlic	Tablespoon	⅔	1	1⅓
Mixed Herbs	Teaspoon	¾	1	1½
Water	Cup	¾	1⅛	1½
Grated Tasty Cheese	Cup	½	¾	1

- Check the 'normal loaf size' for your bread machine in the USING YOUR BREADMAKER section.
- Do not use Time Delay with this recipe.
- Place first eight ingredients in the bread pan in the order recommended in your machine instruction book.
- Fit pan in machine, select Wholemeal Bake Raisin or Sweet cycle and press Start.
- Check liquidity of ingredients.
- Place remaining ingredients in pan when 'beep' sounds, or ten minutes from end of final kneading.
- Remove bread from pan at end of Bake and place on a rack to cool.

Chickpea, wheat and sesame bread

A pleasant nutty taste.

Ingredients	**Measure**	500g (1 lb)	750g (1½ lb)	1kg (2 lb)
Surebake Yeast	Teaspoon	2	3	4
Wholemeal Flour	Cup	1½	2¼	3
Chickpea Flour	Cup	½	¾	1
Gluten Flour	Tablespoon	2	3	4
Salt	Teaspoon	½	¾	1
Lecithin	Tablespoon	1⅓	2	2⅔
Honey	Tablespoon	1⅓	2	2⅔
Milk Powder	Tablespoon	1⅓	2	2⅔
Water	Cup	¾	1⅛	1½
Sesame Seeds	Tablespoon	2	3	4

- Check the 'normal loaf size' for your bread machine in the USING YOUR BREADMAKER section.
- Do not use Time Delay with this recipe.
- Place first nine ingredients in the bread pan in the order recommended in your machine instruction book.
- Fit pan in machine, select Wholemeal Bake Raisin or Sweet cycle and press Start.
- Check liquidity of ingredients.
- Place remaining ingredients in pan when 'beep' sounds, or ten minutes from end of final kneading.
- Remove bread from pan at end of Bake and place on a rack to cool.

George's honey loaf

I love that honey flavour.

Ingredients	Measure	500g (1 lb)	750g (1½ lb)	1kg (2 lb)
Surebake Yeast	Teaspoon	2	3	4
Wholemeal Flour	Cup	2	3	4
Gluten Flour	Tablespoon	1½	2¼	3
Salt	Teaspoon	½	¾	1
Honey	Tablespoon	2	3	4
Lecithin	Tablespoon	1⅓	2	2⅔
Water	Cup	¾	1⅛	1½

- Check the 'normal loaf size' for your bread machine in the USING YOUR BREADMAKER section.
- This recipe can be used with Time Delay.
- Place ingredients in the bread pan in the order recommended in your machine instruction book.
- Fit pan in machine, select Wholemeal Bake cycle and press Start.
- Check liquidity of ingredients.
- Ten minutes from end of Bake, drizzle liquid honey over the top of the loaf.
- Remove bread from pan at end of Bake and place on a rack.

Rye, molasses and wholemeal loaf

Delicious molasses flavour.

Ingredients	Measure	500g (1 lb)	750g (1½ lb)	1kg (2 lb)
Surebake Yeast	Teaspoon	2	3	4
Wholemeal Flour	Cup	1³/₈	2	2¾
Gluten Flour	Tablespoon	2	3	4
Rye Flour	Cup	⁵/₈	1	1¼
Salt	Teaspoon	½	¾	1
Molasses	Tablespoon	2	3	4
Lecithin	Tablespoon	1¹/₃	2	2²/₃
Water	Cup	¾	1¹/₈	1½

- Check the 'normal loaf size' for your bread machine in the USING YOUR BREADMAKER section.
- This recipe can be used with Time Delay.
- Place ingredients in the bread pan in the order recommended in your machine instruction book.
- Fit pan in machine, select Wholemeal Bake cycle and press Start.
- Check liquidity of ingredients.
- Remove bread from pan at end of Bake and place on a rack to cool.

Sour cream loaf

Very very tasty!

Ingredients	Measure	500g (1 lb)	750g (1½ lb)	1kg (2 lb)
Surebake Yeast	Teaspoon	2	3	4
Wholemeal Flour	Cup	2	3	4
Gluten Flour	Tablespoon	1½	2¼	3
Baking Soda	Teaspoon	¼	½	¾
Salt	Teaspoon	½	¾	1
Honey	Tablespoon	1	1½	2
Lecithin	Tablespoon	1¼	2	2¼
Sour Cream	Cup	¾	1	1¼
Egg (measure with water)		1	1	2
Water	Cup	¼	3/8	½

- Check the 'normal loaf size' for your bread machine in the USING YOUR BREADMAKER section.
- Do not use Time Delay with this recipe.
- Place ingredients in the bread pan in the order recommended in your machine instruction book.
- Fit pan in machine, select Wholemeal Bake cycle and press Start.
- Check liquidity of ingredients.
- Remove bread from pan at end of Bake and place on a rack to cool.

Spiced carrot bread

Ooooh, the aroma...

Ingredients	Measure	500g (1 lb)	750g (1½ lb)	1kg (2 lb)
Surebake Yeast	Teaspoon	2	3	4
Wholemeal Flour	Cup	2	3	4
Gluten Flour	Tablespoon	2	3	4
Honey	Tablespoon	1	1½	2
Ground Cloves	Teaspoon	1/4	½	¾
Ground Ginger	Teaspoon	1 1/4	2	2½
Ground Cinnamon	Teaspoon	1	1½	2
Salt	Teaspoon	½	¾	1
Lecithin	Tablespoon	1 1/3	2	2 2/3
Grated Carrots	Cup	½	¾	1
Water	Cup	¾	1 1/8	1½

- Check the 'normal loaf size' for your bread machine in the USING YOUR BREADMAKER section.
- This recipe can be used with Time Delay.
- Place ingredients in the bread pan in the order recommended in your machine instruction book.
- Fit pan in machine, select Wholemeal Bake cycle and press Start.
- Check liquidity of ingredients.
- Remove bread from pan at end of Bake and place on a rack to cool.

Wholemeal, carrot and onion loaf

It's a taste sensation.

Ingredients	**Measure**	500g (1 lb)	750g (1½ lb)	1kg (2 lb)
Surebake Yeast	Teaspoon	2	3	4
Wholemeal Flour	Cup	2	3	4
Gluten Flour	Tablespoon	2	3	4
Salt	Teaspoon	½	¾	1
Lecithin	Tablespoon	1⅓	2	2⅔
Honey	Tablespoon	1⅓	2	2⅔
Milk Powder	Tablespoon	1⅓	2	2⅔
Grated Carrot	Cup	½	¾	1
Chopped Onion	Tablespoon	2	3	4
Parsley	Tablespoon	1	1½	2
Water	Cup	¾	1⅛	1½

- Check the 'normal loaf size' for your bread machine in the USING YOUR BREADMAKER section.
- This recipe can be used with Time Delay.
- Place ingredients in the bread pan in the order recommended in your machine instruction book.
- Fit pan in machine, select Wholemeal Bake cycle and press Start.
- Check liquidity of ingredients.
- Remove bread from pan at end of Bake and place on a rack to cool.

Wholemeal carrot & wheat germ bread

Try this toasted.

Ingredients	**Measure**	500g (1 lb)	750g (1½ lb)	1kg (2 lb)
Surebake Yeast	Teaspoon	2	3	4
Wholemeal Flour	Cup	2	3	4
Gluten Flour	Tablespoon	2	3	4
Wheat Germ	Tablespoon	2¾	4	5½
Salt	Teaspoon	½	¾	1
Lecithin	Tablespoon	1⅓	2	2⅔
Honey	Tablespoon	1⅓	2	2⅔
Grated Carrot	Cup	½	¾	1
Water	Cup	¾	1⅛	1½

- Check the 'normal loaf size' for your bread machine in the USING YOUR BREADMAKER section.
- This recipe can be used with Time Delay.
- Place ingredients in the bread pan in the order recommended in your machine instruction book.
- Fit pan in machine, select Wholemeal Bake cycle and press Start.
- Check liquidity of ingredients.
- Remove bread from pan at end of Bake and place on a rack to cool.

Wholemeal, cornmeal and rye loaf

Great for open sandwiches.

Ingredients	Measure	500g (1 lb)	750g (1½ lb)	1kg (2 lb)
Surebake Yeast	Teaspoon	2	3	4
Rye Flour	Cup	½	¾	1
Wholemeal Flour	Cup	1³/₈	2	2¾
Gluten Flour	Tablespoon	2	3	4
Cornmeal	Tablespoon	2	4	4
Salt	Teaspoon	½	¾	1
Lecithin	Tablespoon	⁷/₈	2	1¾
Water	Cup	1¹/₈	1¼	2¼

- Check the 'normal loaf size' for your bread machine in the USING YOUR BREADMAKER section.
- This recipe can be used with Time Delay.
- Place ingredients in the bread pan in the order recommended in your machine instruction book.
- Fit pan in machine, select Wholemeal Bake cycle and press Start.
- Check liquidity of ingredients.
- Remove bread from pan at end of Bake and place on a rack to cool.

Wholemeal, two fruits and nut bread

A splendid tea bread.

Ingredients	Measure	500g (1 lb)	750g (1½ lb)	1kg (2 lb)
Surebake Yeast	Teaspoon	2	3	4
Wholemeal Flour	Cup	2	3	4
Gluten Flour	Tablespoon	2	3	4
Salt	Teaspoon	½	¾	1
Lecithin	Tablespoon	1⅓	2	2⅔
Cinnamon	Teaspoon	¾	1	1¼
Mashed Banana	Cup	⅝	1	1¼
Water	Cup	⅝	1	1¼
Raisins	Cup	⅜	½	¾
Chopped Nuts	Cup	¼	⅜	½

- Check the 'normal loaf size' for your bread machine in the USING YOUR BREADMAKER section.
- Do not use Time Delay with this recipe.
- Place first eight ingredients in the bread pan in the order recommended in your machine instruction book.
- Fit pan in machine, select Wholemeal Bake Raisin or Sweet cycle and press Start.
- Check liquidity of ingredients.
- Place remaining ingredients in pan when 'beep' sounds, or ten minutes from end of final kneading.
- Remove bread from pan at end of Bake and place on a rack to cool.

Multigrain breads

five

Two scrunchy recipes for the enthusiastic breadmaker driver. Have fun and enjoy the results.

Cracked wheat and oatmeal bread

A dense, nutty taste.

Ingredients	**Measure**	500g (1 lb)	750g (1½ lb)	1kg (2 lb)
Surebake Yeast	Teaspoon	2	3	4
Wholemeal Flour	Cup	1½	2¼	3
Oatmeal	Cup	½	¾	1
Cracked Wheat	Cup	½	¾	1
Gluten Flour	Tablespoon	2	3	4
Salt	Teaspoon	½	¾	1
Honey	Tablespoon	2	3	4
Lecithin	Tablespoon	1½	2¼	3
Water	Cup	¾	1⅛	1½

- Check the 'normal loaf size' for your bread machine in the USING YOUR BREADMAKER section.
- This recipe can be used with Time Delay.
- See 'Cracked Wheat' in Recipes section.
- Place ingredients in the bread pan in the order recommended in your machine instruction book.
- Fit pan in machine, select Basic Bake cycle and press Start.
- Check liquidity of ingredients.
- Remove bread from pan at end of Bake and place on a rack to cool.

Multigrain and sunflower loaf

Just enjoy that oaty crunch.

Ingredients	**Measure**	500g (1 lb)	750g (1½ lb)	1kg (2 lb)
Surebake Yeast	Teaspoon	2	3	4
Wholemeal Flour	Cup	1¾	2⅝	3½
Oat Bran	Cup	¼	⅜	½
Gluten Flour	Tablespoon	2	3	4
Cornmeal	Tablespoon	1⅓	2	2⅔
Salt	Teaspoon	½	¾	1
Honey	Tablespoon	2	3	4
Lecithin	Tablespoon	1⅓	2	2⅔
Water	Cup	1⅛	1¼	2¼
Sunflower Seeds	Tablespoon	2	3	4

- Check the 'normal loaf size' for your bread machine in the USING YOUR BREADMAKER section.
- Do not use Time Delay with this recipe.
- Place first nine ingredients in the bread pan in the order recommended in your machine instruction book.
- Fit pan in machine, select Wholemeal Bake Raisin or Sweet cycle and press Start.
- Check liquidity of ingredients.
- Place remaining ingredients in pan when 'beep' sounds, or ten minutes from end of final kneading.
- Remove bread from pan at end of Bake and place on a rack to cool.

Seven grain loaf

Top with poppy or sesame seeds.

Ingredients	Measure	500g (1 lb)	750g (1½ lb)	1kg (2 lb)
Surebake Yeast	Teaspoon	2	3	4
Wholemeal Flour	Cup	1$^{3}/_{8}$	2	2¾
Seven Grain Flour	Cup	$^{5}/_{8}$	1	1¼
Gluten Flour	Tablespoon	2	3	4
Salt	Teaspoon	¼	½	¾
Honey	Tablespoon	2	3	4
Lecithin	Tablespoon	1	1½	2
Milk Powder	Tablespoon	1$^{1}/_{3}$	2	2$^{2}/_{3}$
Water	Cup	¾	1$^{1}/_{8}$	1½

- Check the 'normal loaf size' for your bread machine in the USING YOUR BREADMAKER section.
- This recipe can be used with Time Delay.
- Place ingredients in the bread pan in the order recommended in your machine instruction book.
- Fit pan in machine, select Basic Bake cycle and press Start.
- Check liquidity of ingredients.
- Remove bread from pan at end of Bake and place on a rack to cool.

High protein breads

six

Because bread is made mainly from cereals, it is low in protein, including some essential acids, as well as low in fats and cholesterol. Growing children need protein, so you can boost the protein quality of a loaf by adding nuts, seeds, egg, cheese or soy flour. Several recipes in the 50/50 and Wholemeal sections are also high in protein. Look for the ones containing cheese. The results are tasty too.

Banana nut loaf

Serve this sliced with a cream cheese spread.

Ingredients	Measure	500g (1 lb)	750g (1½ lb)	1kg (2 lb)
Surebake Yeast	Teaspoon	2	3	4
Wholemeal Flour	Cup	2	3	4
Gluten Flour	Tablespoon	2	3	4
Brown Sugar	Tablespoon	1	1½	2
Salt	Teaspoon	½	¾	1
Lecithin	Tablespoon	1	1½	2
Egg (measure with water)		1	1	2
Mashed Banana	Cup	5/8	1	1¼
Water	Cup	¾	1 1/8	1½
Chopped Nuts	Cup	½	¾	1

- Check the 'normal loaf size' for your bread machine in the USING YOUR BREADMAKER section.
- Do not use Time Delay with this recipe.
- Place first eight ingredients in the bread pan in the order recommended in your machine instruction book.
- Fit pan in machine, select Wholemeal Bake Raisin or Sweet cycle and press Start.
- Check liquidity of ingredients.
- Place remaining ingredients in pan when 'beep' sounds, or ten minutes from end of final kneading.
- Remove bread from pan at end of Bake and place on a rack to cool.

Rosemary and basil egg bread

Superb with spicy dishes.

Ingredients	Measure	500g (1 lb)	750g (1½ lb)	1kg (2 lb)
Surebake Yeast	Teaspoon	2	3	4
Wholemeal Flour	Cup	2	3	4
Gluten Flour	Tablespoon	2	3	4
Brown Sugar	Tablespoon	1	1½	2
Salt	Teaspoon	½	¾	1
Egg (measure with water)		1	2	2
Lecithin	Tablespoon	1	1½	2
Rosemary	Tablespoon	½	¾	1
Basil	Tablespoon	1	1½	2
Water	Cup	¾	1⅛	1½

- Check the 'normal loaf size' for your bread machine in the USING YOUR BREADMAKER section.
- Do not use Time Delay with this recipe.
- Place ingredients in the bread pan in the order recommended in your machine instruction book.
- Fit pan in machine, select Wholemeal Bake cycle and press Start.
- Check liquidity of ingredients.
- Remove bread from pan at end of Bake and place on a rack to cool.

Rye walnut loaf

A subtle walnut flavour.

Ingredients	Measure	500g (1 lb)	750g (1½ lb)	1kg (2 lb)
Surebake Yeast	Teaspoon	2	3	4
Wholemeal Flour	Cup	1½	2¼	3
Rye Flour	Cup	½	¾	1
Gluten Flour	Tablespoon	2	3	4
Milk Powder	Tablespoon	2	3	4
Honey	Tablespoon	1	1½	2
Salt	Teaspoon	½	¾	1
Water	Cup	¾	1⅛	1½
Chopped Walnuts	Cup	⅝	1	1¼

- Check the 'normal loaf size' for your bread machine in the USING YOUR BREADMAKER section.
- Do not use Time Delay with this recipe.
- Place first eight ingredients in the bread pan in the order recommended in your machine instruction book.
- Fit pan in machine, select Wholemeal Bake Raisin or Sweet cycle and press Start.
- Check liquidity of ingredients.
- Place remaining ingredients in pan when 'beep' sounds, or ten minutes from end of final kneading.
- Remove bread from pan at end of Bake and place on a rack to cool.

Sultana caraway bread

A tasty tea bread.

Ingredients	Measure	500g (1 lb)	750g (1½ lb)	1kg (2 lb)
Surebake Yeast	Teaspoon	2	3	4
Wholemeal Flour	Cup	1½	2¼	3
Soy Flour	Cup	½	¾	1
Gluten Flour	Tablespoon	2	3	4
Milk Powder	Tablespoon	2	3	4
Honey	Tablespoon	1	1½	2
Salt	Teaspoon	½	¾	1
Lecithin	Tablespoon	1	1½	2
Water	Cup	¾	1⅛	1½
Caraway Seed	Tablespoon	½	¾	1
Sultanas	Cup	¾	1⅛	1½

- Check the 'normal loaf size' for your bread machine in the USING YOUR BREADMAKER section.
- Do not use Time Delay with this recipe.
- Place first nine ingredients in the bread pan in the order recommended in your machine instruction book.
- Fit pan in machine, select Wholemeal Bake Raisin or Sweet cycle and press Start.
- Check liquidity of ingredients.
- Place remaining ingredients in pan when 'beep' sounds, or ten minutes from end of final kneading.
- Remove bread from pan at end of Bake and place on a rack to cool.

Sunflower and sesame loaf

Oooooh, crunchy!

Ingredients	Measure	500g (1 lb)	750g (1½ lb)	1kg (2 lb)
Surebake Yeast	Teaspoon	2	3	4
Wholemeal Flour	Cup	2	3	4
Gluten Flour	Tablespoon	2	3	4
Sunflower Seed	Tablespoon	2	3	4
Sesame Seed	Tablespoon	2	3	4
Brown Sugar	Tablespoon	1	1½	3
Salt	Teaspoon	½	¾	1
Milk Powder	Tablespoon	2	3	4
Lecithin	Tablespoon	1	1½	2
Water	Cup	7/8	1 3/8	1¾

- Check the 'normal loaf size' for your bread machine in the USING YOUR BREADMAKER section.
- This recipe can be used with Time Delay.
- Place ingredients in the bread pan in the order recommended in your machine instruction book.
- Fit pan in machine, select Wholemeal Bake cycle and press Start.
- Check liquidity of ingredients.
- Remove bread from pan at end of Bake and place on a rack to cool.

Wheat 'n' oats loaf

High protein and high fibre.

Ingredients	**Measure**	500g (1 lb)	750g (1½ lb)	1kg (2 lb)
Surebake Yeast	Teaspoon	2	3	4
Wholemeal Flour	Cup	1³/₈	2	2¾
Rolled Oats	Cup	⅝	1	1¼
Gluten Flour	Tablespoon	2	3	4
Honey	Tablespoon	1½	2¼	3
Salt	Teaspoon	½	¾	1
Milk Powder	Tablespoon	2¾	4	5½
Water	Cup	⅞	1³/₈	1¾

- Check the 'normal loaf size' for your bread machine in the USING YOUR BREADMAKER section.
- This recipe can be used with Time Delay.
- Place ingredients in the bread pan in the order recommended in your machine instruction book.
- Fit pan in machine, select Wholemeal Bake cycle and press Start.
- Check liquidity of ingredients.
- Remove bread from pan at end of Bake and place on a rack to cool.

Soya, linseed and wholemeal bread

Looks good, tastes good, does you good!

Ingredients	**Measure**	500g (1 lb)	750g (1½ lb)	1kg (2 lb)
Surebake Yeast	Teaspoon	2	3	4
High Grade Flour	Cup	5/8	1	1¼
Wholemeal Flour	Cup	1	1½	2
Soya Flour	Cup	3/8	½	¾
Gluten Flour	Tablespoon	1 1/3	2	2 2/3
Brown Sugar	Tablespoon	1	1½	2
Salt	Teaspoon	¼	½	¾
Milk Powder	Tablespoon	1	1½	2
Lecithin	Tablespoon	1	1½	2
Linseeds	Tablespoon	2 2/3	4	5 1/3
Water	Cup	1	1½	2

- Check the 'normal loaf size' for your bread machine in the USING YOUR BREADMAKER section.
- This recipe can be used with Time Delay.
- Place ingredients in the bread pan in the order recommended in your machine instruction book.
- Fit pan in machine, select Wholemeal Bake cycle and press Start.
- Check liquidity, scrape down pan sides with spatula.
- Check liquidity of ingredients.
- Remove bread from pan at end of Bake and place on a rack to cool.

High fibre breads

seven

Bread making cereals are a rich source of both soluble and insoluble fibre (as well as various vitamins and trace elements). Each of the wide range of flours now available has a unique type of fibre.

Most high fibre recipes result in a hearty, dense loaf - great for sandwiches, or in chunks with your soup.

Most high fibre recipes also include gluten to give more lift to your loaf. If you prefer a more dense bread, reduce the gluten quantity. You may need to reduce the liquid slightly as well.

Recipes in the Multigrain section are also high in fibre.

Basic wheat bran bread

Just what the doctor ordered!

Ingredients	**Measure**	500g (1 lb)	750g (1½ lb)	1kg (2 lb)
Surebake Yeast	Teaspoon	2	3	4
Wholemeal Flour	Cup	2	3	4
Gluten Flour	Tablespoon	2	3	4
Wheat Bran	Cup	¼	⅜	½
Salt	Teaspoon	½	¾	1
Lecithin	Tablespoon	1	1½	2
Honey	Tablespoon	2	3	4
Milk Powder	Tablespoon	2	3	4
Water	Cup	¾	1⅛	1½

- Check the 'normal loaf size' for your bread machine in the USING YOUR BREADMAKER section.
- This recipe can be used with Time Delay.
- Place ingredients in the bread pan in the order recommended in your machine instruction book.
- Fit pan in machine, select Wholemeal Bake cycle and press Start.
- Check liquidity of ingredients.
- Remove bread from pan at end of Bake and place on a rack to cool.

Buckwheat and rye loaf

Strong flavours, dense texture.

Ingredients	Measure	500g (1 lb)	750g (1½ lb)	1kg (2 lb)
Surebake Yeast	Teaspoon	2	3	4
Wholemeal Flour	Cup	½	¾	1
Rye Flour	Cup	1	1½	2
Buckwheat Flour	Cup	½	¾	1
Gluten Flour	Tablespoon	2	3	4
Molasses	Tablespoon	1⅓	2	2⅔
Salt	Teaspoon	½	¾	1
Lecithin	Tablespoon	1⅓	2	2⅔
Ground Cloves	Teaspoon	¼	⅜	½
Water	Cup	¾	1⅛	1½

- Check the 'normal loaf size' for your bread machine in the USING YOUR BREADMAKER section.
- Do not use this recipe with Time Delay.
- Place ingredients in the bread pan in the order recommended in your machine instruction book.
- Fit pan in machine, select Wholemeal Bake cycle and press Start.
- Check liquidity of ingredients.
- Remove bread from pan at end of Bake and place on a rack to cool.

Date and molasses loaf

Tasty - slightly sweet.

Ingredients	**Measure**	500g (1 lb)	750g (1½ lb)	1kg (2 lb)
Surebake Yeast	Teaspoon	2	3	4
Wholemeal Flour	Cup	1$^3/_8$	2	2¾
High Grade Flour	Cup	$^5/_8$	1	1¼
Gluten Flour	Tablespoon	1$^1/_3$	2	2$^2/_3$
Molasses	Tablespoon	1	1½	2
Salt	Teaspoon	½	¾	1
Lecithin	Tablespoon	1$^1/_3$	2	2$^2/_3$
Milk Powder	Tablespoon	1$^1/_3$	2	2$^2/_3$
Water	Cup	¾	1$^1/_8$	1½
Chopped Dates	Cup	$^5/_8$	1	1¼

- Check the 'normal loaf size' for your bread machine in the USING YOUR BREADMAKER section.
- Do not use this recipe with Time Delay.
- Place first nine ingredients in the bread pan in the order recommended in your machine instruction book.
- Fit pan in machine, select Wholemeal Bake Raisin or Sweet cycle and press Start.
- Check liquidity of ingredients.
- Place remaining ingredients in pan when 'beep' sounds, or ten minutes from end of final kneading.
- Remove bread from pan at end of Bake and place on a rack to cool.

Fruit bran bread

Tasty and loaded with fruit.

Ingredients	Measure	500g (1 lb)	750g (1½ lb)	1kg (2 lb)
Surebake Yeast	Teaspoon	2	3	4
High Grade Flour	Cup	1	1½	2
Wholemeal Flour	Cup	½	¾	1
Gluten Flour	Tablespoon	1	1½	2
Wheat Bran	Cup	½	¾	1
Milk Powder	Tablespoon	1	1½	2
Lecithin	Tablespoon	1¼	2	2½
Honey	Tablespoon	1¼	2	2½
Salt	Teaspoon	½	¾	1
Water	Cup	¾	1⅛	1½
Raisins	Cup	½	¾	1
Chopped Dates	Cup	½	¾	1

- Check the 'normal loaf size' for your bread machine in the USING YOUR BREADMAKER section.
- Do not use Time Delay with this recipe.
- Place first ten ingredients in the bread pan in the order recommended in your machine instruction book.
- Fit pan in machine, select Basic Bake Raisin cycle and press Start.
- Check liquidity of ingredients.
- Place remaining ingredients in pan when 'beep' sounds, or ten minutes from end of final kneading.
- Remove bread from pan at end of Bake and place on a rack to cool.

Oat bran and wholemeal bread

A delicious oat flavour.

Ingredients	**Measure**	500g (1 lb)	750g (1½ lb)	1kg (2 lb)
Surebake Yeast	Teaspoon	2	3	4
Wholemeal Flour	Cup	2	3	4
Gluten Flour	Tablespoon	2	3	4
Oat Bran	Cup	¼	⅜	½
Salt	Teaspoon	½	¾	1
Lecithin	Tablespoon	1	1½	2
Honey	Tablespoon	2	3	4
Milk Powder	Tablespoon	2	3	4
Water	Cup	¾	1⅛	1½

- Check the 'normal loaf size' for your bread machine in the USING YOUR BREADMAKER section.
- This recipe can be used with Time Delay.
- Place ingredients in the bread pan in the order recommended in your machine instruction book.
- Fit pan in machine, select Wholemeal Bake cycle and press Start.
- Check liquidity of ingredients.
- Remove bread from pan at end of Bake and place on a rack to cool.

Wholemeal and rice bran loaf

Wholemeal taste with a difference.

Ingredients	**Measure**	500g (1 lb)	750g (1½ lb)	1kg (2 lb)
Surebake Yeast	Teaspoon	2	3	4
Wholemeal Flour	Cup	2	3	4
Gluten Flour	Tablespoon	2	3	4
Rice Bran	Cup	¼	⅜	½
Salt	Teaspoon	½	¾	1
Lecithin	Tablespoon	1	1½	2
Rice Syrup	Tablespoon	2	3	4
Milk Powder	Tablespoon	2	3	4
Water	Cup	¾	1⅛	1½

- Check the 'normal loaf size' for your bread machine in the USING YOUR BREADMAKER section.
- Do not use Time Delay with this recipe.
- Place ingredients in the bread pan in the order recommended in your machine instruction book.
- Fit pan in machine, select Wholemeal Bake cycle and press Start.
- Check liquidity of ingredients.
- Remove bread from pan at end of Bake and place on a rack to cool.

Wheat germ wholemeal loaf

Very tasty.

Ingredients	Measure	500g (1 lb)	750g (1½ lb)	1kg (2 lb)
Surebake Yeast	Teaspoon	2	3	4
Wholemeal Flour	Cup	2	3	4
Gluten Flour	Tablespoon	2	3	4
Wheat Germ	Cup	¼	⅜	½
Lecithin	Tablespoon	1	1½	2
Salt	Teaspoon	½	¾	1
Molasses	Tablespoon	2	3	4
Milk Powder	Tablespoon	2	3	4
Water	Cup	¾	1⅛	1½

- Check the 'normal loaf size' for your bread machine in the USING YOUR BREADMAKER section.
- Do not use Time Delay with this recipe.
- Place ingredients in the bread pan in the order recommended in your machine instruction book.
- Fit pan in machine, select Wholemeal Bake cycle and press Start.
- Check liquidity of ingredients.
- Remove bread from pan at end of Bake and place on a rack to cool.

Low salt breads

eight

Sometimes you have to control your salt/sodium intake. The recipes that follow will all help. (Of course any dietary plan you undertake should only be on the advice of your health professional.)

Among other things, salt aids the keeping qualities of yeast bread, so a low salt loaf will not keep well. What a good reason to make fresh bread more often! With your breadmaker, that's no problem.

Cornmeal and wheat germ loaf

Low salt - high fibre.

Ingredients	Measure	500g (1 lb)	750g (1½ lb)	1kg (2 lb)
Surebake Yeast	Teaspoon	1½	2	2½
Wholemeal Flour	Cup	1	1½	2
Gluten Flour	Tablespoon	2	3	4
Cornmeal	Cup	⅝	1	1¼
Wheat Germ	Cup	⅜	½	¾
Sesame Seeds	Tablespoon	2	3	4
Cumin	Teaspoon	½	¾	1
Honey	Tablespoon	1⅓	2	2⅔
Lecithin	Tablespoon	1	1½	2
Water	Cup	¾	1⅛	1½

- Check the 'normal loaf size' for your bread machine in the USING YOUR BREADMAKER section.
- Do not use Time Delay with this recipe.
- Place ingredients in the bread pan in the order recommended in your machine instruction book.
- Fit pan in machine, select Wholemeal Bake cycle and press Start.
- Check liquidity of ingredients.
- Remove bread from pan at end of Bake and place on a rack to cool.

Light wholemeal herb loaf

Low salt - but tasty!

Ingredients	Measure	500g (1 lb)	750g (1½ lb)	1kg (2 lb)
Surebake Yeast	Teaspoon	1	1½	2
High Grade Flour	Cup	1	1½	2
Wholemeal Flour	Cup	1	1½	2
Gluten Flour	Tablespoon	1	1½	2
Honey	Tablespoon	1	1½	2
Lemon Juice	Teaspoon	¾	1	1½
Mixed Herbs	Tablespoon	1⅓	2	2⅔
Olive Oil	Tablespoon	1	1½	2
Water	Cup	⅝	1	1¼

- Check the 'normal loaf size' for your bread machine in the USING YOUR BREADMAKER section.
- Do not use Time Delay with this recipe.
- Place ingredients in the bread pan in the order recommended in your machine instruction book.
- Fit pan in machine, select Basic Bake cycle and press Start.
- Check liquidity of ingredients.
- Remove bread from pan at end of Bake and place on a rack to cool.

Garlic bread

Light garlic flavour.

Ingredients	Measure	500g (1 lb)	750g (1½ lb)	1kg (2 lb)
Surebake Yeast	Teaspoon	1	1½	2
High Grade Flour	Cup	1	1½	2
Wholemeal Flour	Cup	1	1½	2
Gluten Flour	Tablespoon	1⅓	2	2⅔
Minced Garlic	Tablespoon	½	¾	1
Lecithin	Tablespoon	1⅓	2	2⅔
Water	Cup	¾	1⅛	1½

- Check the 'normal loaf size' for your bread machine in the USING YOUR BREADMAKER section.
- This recipe can be used with Time Delay.
- Place ingredients in the bread pan in the order recommended in your machine instruction book.
- Fit pan in machine, select Basic Bake cycle and press Start.
- Check liquidity of ingredients.
- Remove bread from pan at end of Bake and place on a rack to cool.

Salt free multigrain bread

Loaded with protein and flavour.

Ingredients	Measure	500g (1 lb)	750g (1½ lb)	1kg (2 lb)
Surebake Yeast	Teaspoon	1½	2	2½
High Grade Flour	Cup	2	3	4
Milk Powder	Tablespoon	2	3	4
Wheat Bran	Tablespoon	2	3	4
Rolled Oats	Tablespoon	2	3	4
Rye Flour	Tablespoon	2	3	4
Cornmeal	Tablespoon	2	3	4
Honey	Tablespoon	1⅓	2	2⅔
Water	Cup	¾	1⅛	1½

- Check the 'normal loaf size' for your bread machine in the USING YOUR BREADMAKER section.
- Do not use Time Delay with this recipe.
- Place ingredients in the bread pan in the order recommended in your machine instruction book.
- Fit pan in machine, select Wholemeal Bake cycle and press Start.
- Check liquidity of ingredients.
- Remove bread from pan at end of Bake and place on a rack to cool.

Oat bran wholemeal loaf

A light oaty flavour, low salt bread.

Ingredients	**Measure**	500g (1 lb)	750g (1½ lb)	1kg (2 lb)
Surebake Yeast	Teaspoon	1³/₈	2	2¾
Wholemeal Flour	Cup	2	3	4
Oat Bran	Cup	¼	³/₈	½
Gluten Flour	Tablespoon	2	3	4
Honey	Tablespoon	1½	2¼	3
Soy Milk	Cup	¾	1¹/₈	1½

- Check the 'normal loaf size' for your bread machine in the USING YOUR BREADMAKER section.
- This recipe can be used with Time Delay.
- Place ingredients in the bread pan in the order recommended in your machine instruction book.
- Fit pan in machine, select Wholemeal Bake cycle and press Start.
- Check liquidity of ingredients.
- Remove bread from pan at end of Bake and place on a rack to cool.

Pumpkin bread

Spicy and fruity - enjoy!

Ingredients	Measure	500g (1 lb)	750g (1½ lb)	1kg (2 lb)
Surebake Yeast	Teaspoon	1¼	2	2¾
High Grade Flour	Cup	1½	2¼	3
Wholemeal Flour	Cup	½	¾	1
Gluten Flour	Tablespoon	½	¾	1
Lecithin	Tablespoon	1	1½	2
Pumpkin (cooked, drained and mashed)	Cup	½	¾	1
Cinnamon	Teaspoon	1	1½	2
Ginger	Teaspoon	1	1½	2
Sugar	Tablespoon	⅔	1	1⅓
Water	Cup	¾	1⅛	1½
Raisins	Cup	½	¾	1

- Check the 'normal loaf size' for your bread machine in the USING YOUR BREADMAKER section.
- Do not use Time Delay with this recipe.
- Place first ten ingredients in the bread pan in the order recommended in your machine instruction book.
- Fit pan in machine, select Basic Bake cycle and press Start.
- Check liquidity of ingredients.
- Place remaining ingredients in pan when 'beep' sounds, or ten minutes from end of final kneading.
- Remove bread from pan at end of Bake and place on a rack to cool.

Raisin and nut wholemeal loaf

Fruity and low salt.

Ingredients	Measure	500g (1 lb)	750g (1½ lb)	1kg (2 lb)
Surebake Yeast	Teaspoon	1½	2	2¾
Wholemeal Flour	Cup	2	3	4
Gluten Flour	Tablespoon	2	3	4
Lecithin	Tablespoon	1	1½	2
Honey	Tablespoon	1	1½	2
Milk Powder	Tablespoon	1	1½	2
Water	Cup	¾	1⅛	1½
Raisins	Cup	½	¾	1
Chopped Nuts	Cup	¼	⅜	½

- Check the 'normal loaf size' for your bread machine in the USING YOUR BREADMAKER section.
- Do not use Time Delay with this recipe.
- Place first seven ingredients in the bread pan in the order recommended in your machine instruction book.
- Fit pan in machine, select Wholemeal Bake Raisin or Sweet cycle and press Start.
- Check liquidity of ingredients.
- Place remaining ingredients in pan when 'beep' sounds, or ten minutes from end of final kneading.
- Remove bread from pan at end of Bake and place on a rack to cool.

Low sugar and sugar free breads

nine

The recipes in this section use a small amount of fruit or vegetable sugar to help the yeast along and add to the flavour. See the index for Apple and raisin loaf as well.

If you wish, you can make good bread without any sugar (or honey or molasses or syrup) at all. For breads entirely sugar free, see the index for Garlic bread, Tony's favourite loaf and Wheat duo loaf.

Danish raisin bread

Eat it toasted - splendid!

Ingredients	**Measure**	500g (1 lb)	750g (1½ lb)	1kg (2 lb)
Surebake Yeast	Teaspoon	2	3	4
High Grade Flour	Cup	2	3	4
Wheat Germ	Tablespoon	1	1½	2
Milk Powder	Tablespoon	1½	2¼	3
Ground Cardamom	Teaspoon	½	¾	1
Salt	Teaspoon	½	¾	1
Egg (measure with water)		1	2	2
Water	Cup	¾	1⅛	1½
Raisins	Cup	½	¾	1

- Check the 'normal loaf size' for your bread machine in the USING YOUR BREADMAKER section.
- Do not use Time Delay with this recipe.
- Place first eight ingredients in the bread pan in the order recommended in your machine instruction book.
- Fit pan in machine, select Basic Bake Raisin or Sweet cycle and press Start.
- Check liquidity of ingredients.
- Place remaining ingredients in pan when 'beep' sounds, or ten minutes from end of final kneading.
- Remove bread from pan at end of Bake and place on a rack to cool.

Oats and sultana loaf

Try a slice spread with ...

Ingredients	Measure	500g (1 lb)	750g (1½ lb)	1kg (2 lb)
Surebake Yeast	Teaspoon	2	3	4
High Grade Flour	Cup	1⅝	2½	3¼
Rolled Oats	Cup	½	¾	1
Cinnamon	Teaspoon	1	1½	2
Salt	Teaspoon	½	¾	1
Pure Apple Juice	Cup	¾	1⅛	1½
Sultanas	Cup	½	¾	1

- Check the 'normal loaf size' for your bread machine in the USING YOUR BREADMAKER section.
- Do not use Time Delay with this recipe.
- Place first six ingredients in the bread pan in the order recommended in your machine instruction book.
- Fit pan in machine, select Basic Bake Raisin or Sweet cycle and press Start.
- Check liquidity of ingredients.
- Place remaining ingredients in pan when 'beep' sounds, or ten minutes from end of final kneading.
- Remove bread from pan at end of Bake and place on a rack to cool.

Onion rye loaf

Your salad sandwiches will never be the same again!

Ingredients	**Measure**	500g (1 lb)	750g (1½ lb)	1kg (2 lb)
Surebake Yeast	Teaspoon	2	3	4
High Grade Flour	Cup	1½	2¼	3
Rye Flour	Cup	½	¾	1
Salt	Teaspoon	½	¾	1
Raw Onion (minced, drained)	Cup	1	1½	2
Water	Cup	¾	1⅛	1½

- Check the 'normal loaf size' for your bread machine in the USING YOUR BREADMAKER section.
- Do not use Time Delay with this recipe.
- Place ingredients in the bread pan in the order recommended in your machine instruction book.
- Fit pan in machine, select Basic Bake cycle and press Start.
- Check liquidity of ingredients.
- Remove bread from pan at end of Bake and place on a rack to cool.

Gluten free breads

ten

For most of us, bread made from wheat, rye, oats, and barley is an everyday enjoyment. The gluten these cereals contain is an excellent source of protein with the unique ability to hold the gas produced by the yeast during mixing and kneading, allowing the dough to rise and form a loaf. But many of us, for various reasons, are allergic to gluten because it causes a toxic reaction. This section provides some tasty, wholesome, gluten free bread recipes for your breadmaker.

Most folks who have made gluten free bread by hand will know how difficult it is to mix and knead the dough. Actually it's more a batter than a dough - very sticky and almost impossible to handle. If ever there was a job tailor-made for the bread machine, this is it. The result is still a low cost homemade bread, fresh when you want it, with the bonus that no ingredients are contaminated by wheat products. All this without getting your hands sticky. Marvellous!

Take note of these tips when using the recipes in this section.

- *Gluten free bread batter is heavy. Choose a loaf size smaller than the full capacity (normal loaf size) of your breadmaker. If the capacity is 1kg (2lb), keep the loaf size to not more than 750g (1½lb). Erring on the side of caution will prevent overloading the motor and also avoid batter overflows.*
- *Gluten free dough uses more liquid than regular dough. It resembles a thick batter. Check the mix often, after one or two loaves you will soon get to know how a good mix looks. Don't be afraid to adjust it with flour or water as required.*
- *The recipe will mix more easily if you put the liquids in the pan first, even if your machine instructions say otherwise.*
- *Gluten free recipes use more yeast than similar wheat bread recipes.*
- *Use only active dried yeast in these recipes, not Surebake yeast.*
- *If your machine has a yeast dispenser, do not use it. Just sprinkle the yeast on top of the dry ingredients in the pan.*
- *I find that a combination of flours, as in these recipes, gives more flavour, but feel free to experiment with your own combination.*
- *Check when buying from open bins - contamination from nearby wheat products can easily happen.*
- *If you have an allergy, contact one of the many support groups for dietary advice suitable for your condition . Ask your health professional for contact names and addresses.*
- *Use the additives 'Xanthane' or 'Guar Gum' strictly as given in the recipes. Do not throw Guar Gum in ad lib because excessive amounts can have a slight laxative effect.*

Apple bread

Try it toasted.

Ingredients	Measure	500g (1 lb)	750g (1½ lb)	1kg (2 lb)
Active Dried Yeast	Teaspoon	3¼	4¾	6¼
Guar Gum or Xanthane	Teaspoon	2¾	4	5½
White Rice Flour	Cup	1⅝	2½	3¼
Tapioca Flour	Cup	1	1½	2
Honey	Tablespoon	2¾	4	5½
Salt	Teaspoon	½	¾	1
Apple Sauce	Cup	⅝	1	1¼
Cinnamon	Teaspoon	½	¾	1
Soy Milk	Cup	⅞	1⅜	1¾
Apple (peeled and chopped small)	Cup	⅝	1	1¼

- Choose a loaf size smaller than the 'normal loaf size' for your breadmaker. See the USING YOUR BREADMAKER section.
- Do not use Time Delay with this recipe.
- Place first nine ingredients in the bread pan in the order recommended.
- Fit pan in machine, select Wholemeal Raisin Bake cycle and press Start.
- Scrape ingredients adhering to pan into mixture with rubber spatula.
- Check liquidity of ingredients.
- Place remaining ingredients in pan when 'beep' sounds, or ten minutes from end of final kneading.
- Remove bread from pan at end of Bake and place on a rack to cool.

Banana loaf

Loaded with good things.

Ingredients	Measure	500g (1 lb)	750g (1½ lb)	1kg (2 lb)
Active Dried Yeast	Teaspoon	3¼	4¾	6¼
Guar Gum or Xanthane	Teaspoon	2	3	4
Brown Rice Flour	Cup	1³/₈	2	2¾
Chickpea Flour	Cup	³/₈	½	¾
Rice Bran	Cup	³/₈	½	¾
Sugar	Tablespoon	2¾	4	5½
Salt	Teaspoon	½	¾	1
Sesame Seed	Tablespoon	1¹/₃	2	2²/₃
Milk Powder	Cup	³/₈	½	¾
Egg (measure with water)		1	2	3
Banana (mashed)	Cup	⁵/₈	1	1¼
Water	Cup	1¼	1⁷/₈	2½

- Choose a loaf size smaller than the 'normal loaf size' for your breadmaker. See the USING YOUR BREADMAKER section.
- Do not use Time Delay with this recipe.
- Place ingredients in the bread pan in the order recommended.
- Fit pan in machine, select Wholemeal Bake cycle and press Start.
- Scrape ingredients adhering to pan into mixture with rubber spatula.
- Check liquidity of ingredients.
- Remove bread from pan at end of Bake and place on a rack to cool.

Basic white loaf

A great taste.

Ingredients	Measure	500g (1 lb)	750g (1½ lb)	1kg (2 lb)
Active Dried Yeast	Teaspoon	3¼	4¾	6¼
Guar Gum or Xanthane	Teaspoon	2	3	4
White Rice Flour	Cup	1⅜	2	2¾
Potato Starch Flour	Cup	⅜	½	¾
Chickpea Flour	Cup	⅜	½	¾
Sugar	Tablespoon	2¾	4	5½
Salt	Teaspoon	½	¾	1
Lecithin	Tablespoon	2	3	4
Milk Powder	Tablespoon	2	3	4
Egg (measure with water)		2	3	4
Vinegar (white)	Teaspoon	¾	1	1¼
Water	Cup	1⅜	2	2¾

- Choose a loaf size smaller than the 'normal loaf size' for your breadmaker. See the USING YOUR BREADMAKER section.
- Do not use Time Delay with this recipe.
- Place ingredients in the bread pan in the order recommended.
- Fit pan in machine, select Wholemeal Bake cycle and press Start.
- Scrape ingredients adhering to pan into mixture with rubber spatula.
- Check liquidity of ingredients.
- Remove bread from pan at end of Bake and place on a rack to cool.

Four flour loaf

Splendid for sandwiches.

Ingredients	Measure	500g (1 lb)	750g (1½ lb)	1kg (2 lb)
Active Dried Yeast	Teaspoon	3¼	4¾	6¼
Guar Gum or Xanthane	Teaspoon	2¾	4	5½
Brown Rice Flour	Cup	1⅜	2	2¾
Soy Flour	Cup	⅝	1	1¼
Potato Starch Flour	Cup	⅜	½	¾
Tapioca Flour	Cup	⅜	½	¾
Sugar	Tablespoon	2¾	4	5½
Salt	Teaspoon	¾	1	1¼
Egg (measure with milk)		1	2	3
Soy Milk	Cup	1½	2¼	3

- Choose a loaf size smaller than the 'normal loaf size' for your breadmaker. See the USING YOUR BREADMAKER section.
- Do not use Time Delay with this recipe.
- Place ingredients in the bread pan in the order recommended.
- Fit pan in machine, select Wholemeal Bake cycle and press Start.
- Scrape ingredients adhering to pan into mixture with rubber spatula.
- Check liquidity of ingredients.
- Remove bread from pan at end of Bake and place on a rack to cool.

Honeyed egg bread

Honey and egg? Delicious together.

Ingredients	Measure	500g (1 lb)	750g (1½ lb)	1kg (2 lb)
Active Dried Yeast	Teaspoon	3¼	4¾	6¼
Guar Gum or Xanthane	Teaspoon	2¼	3½	4½
White Rice Flour	Cup	1⅜	2	2¾
Tapioca Flour	Cup	1	1½	2
Honey	Tablespoon	2¾	4	5½
Salt	Teaspoon	¾	1	1¼
Lecithin	Tablespoon	2¾	4	5½
Egg (measure with water)		2	3	4
Soy Milk	Cup	1⅝	2½	3¼

- Choose a loaf size smaller than the 'normal loaf size' for your breadmaker. See the USING YOUR BREADMAKER section.
- Do not use Time Delay with this recipe.
- Place ingredients in the bread pan in the order recommended.
- Fit pan in machine, select Wholemeal Bake cycle and press Start.
- Scrape ingredients adhering to pan into mixture with rubber spatula.
- Check liquidity of ingredients.
- Remove bread from pan at end of Bake and place on a rack to cool.

Peanut rice loaf

Oooooh, that aroma!

Ingredients	Measure	500g (1 lb)	750g (1½ lb)	1kg (2 lb)
Active Dried Yeast	Teaspoon	3¼	4¾	6¼
Guar Gum or Xanthane	Teaspoon	2¼	3½	4½
Brown Rice Flour	Cup	1³/₈	2	2¾
Tapioca Flour	Cup	½	¾	1
Potato Starch Flour	Cup	½	¾	1
Sugar	Tablespoon	1¹/₃	2	2²/₃
Salt	Teaspoon	¾	1	1¼
Peanut Butter	Cup	³/₈	½	¾
Lecithin	Tablespoon	²/₃	1	1¹/₃
Water	Cup	1½	2¼	3

- Choose a loaf size smaller than the 'normal loaf size' for your breadmaker. See the USING YOUR BREADMAKER section.
- Do not use Time Delay with this recipe.
- Place ingredients in the bread pan in the order recommended.
- Fit pan in machine, select Wholemeal Bake cycle and press Start.
- Scrape ingredients adhering to pan into mixture with rubber spatula.
- Check liquidity of ingredients.
- Remove bread from pan at end of Bake and place on a rack to cool.

Raisin bran loaf

Sweet and crunchy.

Ingredients	Measure	500g (1 lb)	750g (1½ lb)	1kg (2 lb)
Active Dried Yeast	Teaspoon	3¼	4¾	6¼
Guar Gum or Xanthane	Teaspoon	2¾	4	5½
Brown Rice Flour	Cup	1⅜	2	2¾
Rice Bran	Cup	⅝	1	1¼
Chickpea Flour	Cup	⅜	½	¾
Potato Starch Flour	Cup	⅜	½	¾
Honey	Tablespoon	2	3	4
Salt	Teaspoon	1	1½	2
Soy Milk	Cup	1¼	1¾	2½
Raisins	Cup	⅜	1	1¼
Pumpkin Seeds	Cup	¼	⅜	½

- Choose a loaf size smaller than the 'normal loaf size' for your breadmaker. See the USING YOUR BREADMAKER section.
- Do not use Time Delay with this recipe.
- Place first nine ingredients in the bread pan in the order recommended.
- Fit pan in machine, select Wholemeal Raisin Bake cycle and press Start.
- Scrape ingredients adhering to pan into mixture with rubber spatula.
- Check liquidity of ingredients.
- Place remaining ingredients in pan when 'beep' sounds, or ten minutes from end of final kneading.
- Remove bread from pan at end of Bake and place on a rack to cool.

Rice and tapioca loaf

Good texture and flavour.

Ingredients	**Measure**	500g (1 lb)	750g (1½ lb)	1kg (2 lb)
Active Dried Yeast	Teaspoon	3¼	4¾	6¼
Guar Gum or Xanthane	Teaspoon	2¼	3½	4½
White Rice Flour	Cup	1½	2¼	3
Tapioca Flour	Cup	¾	1⅛	1½
Honey	Tablespoon	2¾	4	5½
Salt	Teaspoon	1	1½	2
Lecithin	Tablespoon	2	3	4
Milk Powder	Cup	½	¾	1
Egg (measure with water)		2	3	4
Vinegar (white)	Teaspoon	¾	1	1¼
Water	Cup	1½	2¼	3

- Choose a loaf size smaller than the 'normal loaf size' for your breadmaker. See the USING YOUR BREADMAKER section.
- Do not use Time Delay with this recipe.
- Place ingredients in the bread pan in the order recommended.
- Fit pan in machine, select Wholemeal Bake cycle and press Start.
- Scrape ingredients adhering to pan into mixture with rubber spatula.
- Check liquidity of ingredients.
- Remove bread from pan at end of Bake and place on a rack to cool.

Sultana and raisin loaf

Try it toasted.

Ingredients	Measure	500g (1 lb)	750g (1½ lb)	1kg (2 lb)
Active Dried Yeast	Teaspoon	3¼	4¾	6¼
Guar Gum or Xanthane	Teaspoon	2¼	3½	4½
Brown Rice Flour	Cup	1⅜	2	2¾
Soy Flour	Cup	½	¾	1
Potato Starch Flour	Cup	½	¾	1
Brown Sugar	Tablespoon	2	3	4
Salt	Teaspoon	¾	1	1¼
Lecithin	Tablespoon	2	3	4
Soy Milk	Cup	1⅜	2	2¾
Raisins	Cup	¼	⅜	½
Sultanas	Cup	¼	⅜	3¼

- Choose a loaf size smaller than the 'normal loaf size' for your breadmaker. See the USING YOUR BREADMAKER section.
- Do not use Time Delay with this recipe.
- Place first nine ingredients in the bread pan in the order recommended.
- Fit pan in machine, select Wholemeal Raisin Bake cycle and press Start.
- Scrape ingredients adhering to pan into mixture with rubber spatula.
- Check liquidity of ingredients.
- Place remaining ingredients in pan when 'beep' sounds, or ten minutes from end of final kneading.
- Remove bread from pan at end of Bake and place on a rack to cool.

Yoghurt herb bread

Delicious with cheese.

Ingredients	Measure	500g (1 lb)	750g (1½ lb)	1kg (2 lb)
Active Dried Yeast	Teaspoon	3¼	4¾	6¼
Guar Gum or Xanthane	Teaspoon	2¾	4	5½
White Rice Flour	Cup	1⅜	2	2¾
Tapioca Flour	Cup	⅜	½	¾
Potato Starch Flour	Cup	⅜	½	¾
Chickpea Flour	Cup	⅝	1	1¼
Mixed Herbs	Teaspoon	2	3	4
Sugar	Tablespoon	2	3	4
Salt	Teaspoon	¾	1	1¼
Plain Yoghurt	Cup	½	¾	1
Milk	Cup	1	1½	2
Baking Soda	Teaspoon	¼	½	¾

- Choose a loaf size smaller than the 'normal loaf size' for your breadmaker. See the USING YOUR BREADMAKER section.
- Do not use Time Delay with this recipe.
- Place ingredients in the bread pan in the order recommended.
- Fit pan in machine, select Wholemeal Bake cycle and press Start.
- Scrape ingredients adhering to pan into mixture with rubber spatula.
- Check liquidity of ingredients.
- Remove bread from pan at end of Bake and place on a rack to cool.

Wheat free breads

eleven

People with a wheat allergy react adversely to some proteins found only in wheat products. Fortunately a variety of non-wheat flours can be substituted in several recipes.

All the gluten free recipes in this book are also wheat free.

Banana wheat free loaf

Delightful!

Ingredients	Measure	500g (1 lb)	750g (1½ lb)	1kg (2 lb)
Active Dried Yeast	Teaspoon	2	3	4
Oatmeal	Cup	⅝	1	1¼
Potato Starch	Cup	½	¾	1
Rolled Oats	Cup	½	¾	1
Rice Flour	Cup	⅜	½	¾
Guar Gum	Teaspoon	2	3	4
Honey	Tablespoon	1½	2¼	3
Salt	Teaspoon	½	¾	1
Cinnamon	Teaspoon	½	¾	1
Mashed Banana	Cup	⅝	1	1¼
Soy Milk	Cup	¾	1⅛	1½

- Check the 'normal loaf size' for your bread machine in the USING YOUR BREADMAKER section.
- Do not use Time Delay with this recipe.
- Place ingredients in the bread pan in the order recommended in your machine instruction book.
- Fit pan in machine, select Wholemeal Bake cycle and press Start.
- Scrape ingredients adhering to pan into mixture with rubber spatula.
- Check liquidity of ingredients.
- Remove bread from pan at end of Bake and place on a rack to cool.

Barley and rye bread

Wheat free - with a splendid barley taste.

Ingredients	**Measure**	500g (1 lb)	750g (1½ lb)	1kg (2 lb)
Active Dried Yeast	Teaspoon	2	3	4
Barley Flour	Cup	1	1½	2
Rye Flour	Cup	½	¾	1
Rice Flour	Cup	½	¾	1
Guar Gum	Teaspoon	2	3	4
Molasses	Tablespoon	2	3	4
Salt	Teaspoon	1	1½	2
Lecithin	Tablespoon	1	1½	2
Soy Milk	Cup	¾	1⅛	1½

- Check the 'normal loaf size' for your bread machine in the USING YOUR BREADMAKER section.
- Do not use Time Delay with this recipe.
- Place ingredients in the bread pan in the order recommended in your machine instruction book.
- Fit pan in machine, select Wholemeal Bake cycle and press Start.
- Scrape ingredients adhering to pan into mixture with rubber spatula.
- Check liquidity of ingredients.
- Remove bread from pan at end of Bake and place on a rack to cool.

Oat and cornmeal with sesame

Lots of protein and fibre, and wheat free.

Ingredients	Measure	500g (1 lb)	750g (1½ lb)	1kg (2 lb)
Active Dried Yeast	Teaspoon	2	3	4
Oatmeal	Cup	1	1½	2
Cornmeal	Cup	½	¾	1
Barley Flour	Cup	½	¾	1
Guar Gum	Teaspoon	2	3	4
Honey	Tablespoon	2	3	4
Salt	Teaspoon	1	1½	2
Sesame Seed	Tablespoon	1½	2¼	2
Lecithin	Tablespoon	1	1½	2
Egg (measure with water)		1	2	2
Water	Cup	1	1½	2

- Check the 'normal loaf size' for your bread machine in the USING YOUR BREADMAKER section.
- Do not use Time Delay with this recipe.
- Place ingredients in the bread pan in the order recommended in your machine instruction book.
- Fit pan in machine, select Wholemeal Bake cycle and press Start.
- Scrape ingredients adhering to pan into mixture with rubber spatula.
- Check liquidity of ingredients.
- Remove bread from pan at end of Bake and place on a rack to cool.

Milk/lactose free breads

twelve

People with an allergy to lactose must totally avoid cow's milk, fresh or dried. Although milk is used in bread making to add calcium and protein and to soften the texture, it is no problem to make good bread in your breadmaker without any milk at all.

See also George's basic test loaf and Good English bread in the Basic Breads section. Both are lactose free recipes

Almond bread

A machine version of Pain d'Amandes. Try it with apricot jam.

Ingredients	**Measure**	500g (1 lb)	750g (1½ lb)	1kg (2 lb)
Surebake Yeast	Teaspoon	2	3	4
High Grade Flour	Cup	2	3	4
Brown Sugar	Tablespoon	2¾	4	5½
Salt	Teaspoon	1	1½	2
Lecithin	Tablespoon	2¾	4	5½
Ground Almonds	Cup	½	¾	1
Almond Essence	Teaspoon	½	¾	1
Cinnamon	Teaspoon	½	¾	1
Water	Cup	¾	1⅛	1½

- Check the 'normal loaf size' for your bread machine in the USING YOUR BREADMAKER section.
- Do not use Time Delay with this recipe.
- Place ingredients in the bread pan in the order recommended in your machine instruction book.
- Fit pan in machine, select Basic Bake cycle and press Start.
- Check liquidity of ingredients.
- Remove bread from pan at end of Bake and place on a rack to cool.

Tony's favourite loaf

No fat, sugar, or salt - divine flavour!

Ingredients	Measure	500g (1 lb)	750g (1½ lb)	1kg (2 lb)
Surebake Yeast	Teaspoon	2	3	4
High Grade Flour	Cup	1	1½	2
Wholemeal Flour	Cup	1	1½	2
Gluten Flour	Tablespoon	1	1½	2
Pure Apple Juice	Cup	¾	1⅛	1½

- Check the 'normal loaf size' for your bread machine in the USING YOUR BREADMAKER section.
- This recipe can be used with Time Delay.
- Place ingredients in the bread pan in the order recommended in your machine instruction book.
- Fit pan in machine, select Basic Bake cycle and press Start.
- Check liquidity of ingredients.
- Remove bread from pan at end of Bake and place on a rack to cool.

Wheat duo loaf

Wheat and buckwheat - different - tasty.

Ingredients	**Measure**	500g (1 lb)	750g (1½ lb)	1kg (2 lb)
Surebake Yeast	Teaspoon	2	3	4
Wholemeal Flour	Cup	1½	2¼	3
Buckwheat Flour	Cup	½	¾	1
Gluten Flour	Tablespoon	2	3	4
Salt	Teaspoon	½	¾	1
Egg (measure with juice)		1	1	2
Pure Apple Juice	Cup	¾	1⅛	1½

- Check the 'normal loaf size' for your bread machine in the USING YOUR BREADMAKER section.
- Do not use Time Delay with this recipe.
- Place ingredients in the bread pan in the order recommended in your machine instruction book.
- Fit pan in machine, select Wholemeal Bake cycle and press Start.
- Check liquidity of ingredients.
- Remove bread from pan at end of Bake and place on a rack to cool.

'Before bake' toppings

Just before 'Bake' starts:

- Open breadmaker lid and, with a pastry brush, coat the top of the loaf with a little milk, olive oil or egg wash.
- Sprinkle on your selection from:

chopped nuts	chopped olives
chopped onion	chopped sundried tomatoes
desiccated coconut	grated cheese
rolled oats	sugar crystals
poppy seeds	pumpkin seeds
sunflower seeds	sesame seeds
sea salt	

- For a shiny golden crust just coat with egg wash only.
- Close lid and your breadmaker will complete the job for you.

Egg wash

Egg	Whole	1
Sugar	Teaspoon	1
Water	Tablespoon	1

Beat together and brush on as required in recipe.

Glazes

Use to decorate or add to the crust flavour.

- Stand finished loaf on wire rack to cool.
- When cool stand rack and loaf on a tray to collect spillage.
- Drizzle or spoon the selected glaze over the loaf until it is coated to your satisfaction.

Place ingredients in blender and combine till smooth and thin enough to drizzle.

Chocolate glaze

Butter (soft)	Tablespoon	2
Icing Sugar	Cup	2/3
Cocoa	Tablespoon	1
Vanilla Essence	Teaspoon	½
Milk	Tablespoon	1

Coconut glaze

Icing Sugar	Cup	¾
Butter (melted)	Teaspoon	3
Vanilla Essence	Teaspoon	½
Desiccated Coconut	Tablespoon	4
Hot Water	Tablespoon	4

Citrus glaze

Icing Sugar	Cup	½
Grated Lemon Rind	Teaspoon	1
Grated Orange Rind	Teaspoon	1
Lemon Juice	Tablespoon	1

Spicy glaze

Icing Sugar	Cup	½
Allspice	Teaspoon	¼
Ground Cinnamon	Teaspoon	¼
Water	Tablespoon	1

Vanilla glaze

Icing Sugar	Cup	½
Vanilla Essence	Teaspoon	½
Milk	Teaspoon	2

'After bake' spreads, toppings & butters

- Use to 'dress up' a finished loaf as a tasty frosting.
- Spread on slices of a fresh baked loaf.
- As a base in a sandwich.
- As a filling on their own in a thinly sliced cocktail sandwich.
- Spread on canapes as a base for other savoury items.
- Try slicing a loaf horizontally and spreading thickly before reassembly.
- Use as a dip.

Spreads

Process in blender at medium speed until soft and fluffy:

Avocado mexican		
Avocado	Teaspoon	1
Lemon Juice	Tablespoon	2
Salsa	Cup	1

Chocolate and Banana

Mashed Ripe Banana	Cup	½
Melted Chocolate Pieces	Cup	½

Fruit Cream Cheese

Cream Cheese (soft)	Cup	¾
Full Fruit Jam (to taste)	Cup	¼

Ham and Cheese

Cream Cheese (soft)	Cup	¾
Fine Chopped Ham	Tablespoon	2
Grated Tasty Cheese	Tablespoon	1
Mustard (prepared)	Teaspoon	½

Herb and Cream Cheese

Cream Cheese (soft)	Cup	¾
Mixed Dried Herbs	Teaspoon	1
Minced Garlic	Teaspoon	1

Honey and Orange

Butter	Cup	¾
Honey	Tablespoon	2
Grated Orange Rind	Teaspoon	2

Honey and Walnut

Cream Cheese (soft)	Cup	¾
Chopped Walnuts	Tablespoon	1
Honey	Tablespoon	1

Toppings

Process in blender at medium speed until soft and fluffy.

Cream Cheese

Cream Cheese (soft)	Cup	¾
Milk	Tablespoon	1
Vanilla Essence	Teaspoon	½
Icing Sugar	Cup	1
Salt	Teaspoon	¼

Put sugar and water in a saucepan, boil while stirring, cool and add rum. Spoon over bread when serving.

Rum Syrup

Sugar	Cup	1
Water	Cup	½
Rum	Cup	½

Butters

Combine in a bowl, then cool until required:

Cheese and Herb

Butter (soft)	Cup	¾
Parmesan Cheese	Tablespoon	1
Dried Parsley	Teaspoon	1
Dried Oregano	Teaspoon	¼
Garlic Salt	Teaspoon	¼

Cinnamon

Butter (soft)	Cup	½
Castor Sugar	Tablespoon	2
Ground Cinnamon	Tablespoon	2

Curry butter

Butter (soft)	Cup	¾
Fine Chopped Shallot	Tablespoon	2
Salt	Teaspoon	½
Cayenne Pepper	Teaspoon	½
Curry Powder	Tablespoon	2

Garlic butter

Butter (soft)	Cup	¾
Minced Garlic	Teaspoon	2
Tabasco Sauce	Drops	2
Dried Mixed Herbs	Teaspoon	½

Ginger and Nut

Butter (soft)	Cup	¾
Ground Ginger	Tablespoon	1½
Fine Ground Nuts	Cup	½
Brown Sugar	Tablespoon	1
Allspice	Teaspoon	½

Golden Syrup

Butter (soft)	Cup	½
Brown Sugar	Tablespoon	1
Golden Syrup	Tablespoon	2
Lemon Juice	Teaspoon	¼

Herb

Butter (soft)	Cup	¾
Mixed Dried Herbs	Teaspoon	2
Salt	To Taste	
Black Pepper	To Taste	
Lemon Juice	Teaspoon	1

Horseradish

Butter (soft)	Cup	½
Horseradish Cream	Tablespoon	2
Vinegar	Teaspoon	½
Honey	Teaspoon	1

Marmite/Vegemite

Butter (soft)	Cup	½
Marmite or Vegemite	Teaspoon (or to taste)	2

Lemon

Butter (soft)	Cup	¾
Lemon Juice	Teaspoon	2
Grated Lemon Rind	Teaspoon	1
White Pepper	To Taste	

Mustard

Butter (soft)	Cup	¾
Mustard (prepared)	Teaspoon	3
Black Pepper	Teaspoon	½

My gran's sandwich

Butter (soft)	Cup	½
Lemon Juice	Teaspoon	2
Black Pepper	Teaspoon	½
Parsley (chop fine)	Tablespoon	1

about unexpected results

'Who makes no mistakes does not usually make anything.' E.J. Phelps (1828-1900)

Your breadmaker has presented you with a failure. Go on, be in the majority, blame the machine first, then maybe the recipe - it's the usual reaction.

In my experience the blame seldom lies with either of these suspects. Less than 20 per cent of the machines brought to me for servicing over the past ten years actually turn out to have a defect, and a large number of those defects can be put down to fair wear and tear or actual physical damage, for example, where a machine has fallen from a bench top. Very few of the breadmakers have actual circuit or programme defects.

Recipes can sometimes be blamed, but generally only if they are new or untried, still requiring a little fine tuning. Most published recipes, including those you find in this book, have been well tried in many different kinds of breadmakers. Therefore, it is reasonably true to say that, short of a misprint, you can generally rule out the recipe itself as being to blame for a poor result.

In this section I have attempted to bring together most of the possible and probable reasons why your efforts have not quite produced the bread you expected. About 80 per cent of unexpected results originate in the area of machine breadmaking I call 'the variables'. *These variables include:*

- Ingredients which are unsuitable for the programme you are using, or are stale;
- Incorrect measurements - either too little or too much;
- Wrong choice of programme;
- Interference with the proper operation of the machine;
- Environment;
- Power supply;
- Driver error.

Therefore, before you abandon your breadmaker completely or call in a serviceperson, think the problem through and check all possible reasons that could account for your results.

In the following examples of results and possible causes, some events may seem a trifle naive, but they actually happened.

Unmixed, uncooked, in fact just as you left it when you put the ingredients in:

- Did you push the Start button?
- Was power interrupted after starting?

Mixed and risen, but not cooked:

- 'Dough' mode selected instead of 'Bread'?
- Power interrupted?

- 'Stop' or 'Reset' button pushed after starting?
- Was the lid opened repeatedly, or left open? If you really can't contain your curiosity perhaps you should have a breadmaker with a window in the lid! Keep an eye on the children. Remember that childhood and curiosity go together. (And on occasion the machine gets very hot.)

The loaf sides are partly browned, partly floury and the centre partly cooked and sticky:

- Too much liquid used. Did you make allowance for the liquidity of other ingredients, grains, fruit etc?
- Was the lid opened repeatedly?
- Was the power supply interrupted?

The loaf has a mushroom-shaped top coming over the top of the pan:

- Too much yeast used?
- Too much sugar?
- Was fruit added without reducing sugar?

Crust not browned:

- Lid opened during baking?
- Wrong programme selected?

Crust heavy and over browned:

- Too much sugar?
- Crust control set too high?

Not baked in centre:

- Not enough flour used?
- Too much liquid?

Dense, heavy texture:

- Too much flour used?
- Not enough sugar?
- Not enough liquid?
- Not enough yeast?
- Too much of other dry ingredients, grains, fruit, etc?

Texture coarse and full of holes:

- Too much liquid?
- Salt left out?
- Too much sugar?
- Too much yeast?
- Environment too hot? Keep the breadmaker clear of walls and other objects.

Risen too much:

- Too much flour?
- Too much yeast?
- Too much sugar?
- Too much liquid?

Heavy, collapsed top:

- Too much liquid?
- Too much sugar?
- Not enough salt?

Not risen enough:

- Not enough yeast?
- Incorrect type of yeast used?
- Too much liquid?
- Not enough sugar?
- Too much salt?
- Stale flour used?
- Self raising flour used?
- Ingredients placed in bread pan in incorrect order?

Sides of loaf caved in and moist inside:

- Left in pan too long after baking?

Slicing uneven - too soft:

- Allow at least 30 minutes to cool after removing loaf from the pan.

All action has stopped part way through the kneading process:

- Is the environment too hot?
- Is anything blocking the vent on the side and top of the machine?

An unrisen, unmixed but well baked mess?

- Did you remember to replace the kneader blade in the pan?

Still got a problem ?

- See **HELP !** at the end of this book.

Table 1

Quantities in relation to normal loaf size

(nominal capacity)

Use for either cup or tablespoon or teaspoon metric measures

NORMAL LOAF SIZE

500g (1 lb)	750g (1½ lb)	1kg (2 lb)	1.25kg (2½ lb)	1.5kg (3 lb)
1/8	3/16	¼	5/16	3/8
¼	3/8	½	5/8	¾
3/8	½	¾	7/8	1 1/8
½	¾	1	1¼	1½
5/8	1	1¼	1 5/8	2
¾	1 1/8	1½	1 7/8	2¼
7/8	1 3/8	1¾	2¼	2¾
1	1½	2	2½	3
1 1/8	1¾	2¼	2 7/8	3½
1¼	1 7/8	2½	3 1/8	3¾

500g (1 lb)	750g (1½ lb)	1kg (2 lb)	1.25kg (2½ lb)	1.5kg (3 lb)
1⅜	2	2¾	3⅜	4
1½	2¼	3	3¾	4½
1⅝	2½	3¼	4⅛	5
1¾	2⅝	3½	4⅜	5¼
1⅞	2¾	3¾	4⅝	5½
2	3	4	5	6

- Adjust to nearest logical amount

To convert a recipe from one loaf size to another, find the ingredient quantity in the loaf size you know and read off the loaf size you require on the same line – using the same cup or tablespoon or teaspoon metric.

Table 2

Most commonly used ingredients - weights for volume

In international metric grams and cups

Ingredients	Metric Cup / Parts	1/4	3/8	½	5/8	¾	7/8	1
Jam, Mashed Pumpkin	Grams	90	105	155	205	250	295	345
Honey, Golden Syrup		90	105	155	205	250	295	345
Molasses		90	105	155	205	250	295	345
Sultanas		30	55	90	105	125	140	155
Currants		30	55	90	105	125	140	155
Raisins		30	55	90	105	125	140	155
Chopped Dried Fruit		30	55	90	105	125	140	155
Corn, Ground Almonds		45	60	75	105	125	140	155
Rice, Hazelnuts		45	60	75	105	125	140	155
Whole Grains		45	60	75	105	125	140	155
Coarsely Chopped Nuts		45	60	75	105	125	140	155

Ingredients	**Metric Cup / Parts**	1/4	3/8	½	5/8	¾	7/8	1
Finely Grated Cheeses	**Grams**	30	45	65	80	95	110	125
Kibbled Grains, Milk Powder		30	45	65	80	95	110	125
Finely Chopped Nuts, Icing Sugar		30	45	65	80	95	110	125
High Grade Flour, Peanuts		40	55	75	95	110	130	150
Wholemeal Flours		40	55	75	95	110	130	150
Crumbs (dried)		40	55	75	95	110	130	150
Coarsely Grated Cheeses, Half Walnuts		25	35	45	60	70	80	90
Rolled Oats, Desiccated Coconut		25	35	45	60	70	80	90
Brown Sugar, Butter		45	65	90	105	125	150	170
White Sugar, Rice, Water		60	94	125	156	185	220	250
Mashed Potato		65	95	130	160	195	225	255
Milk, Yoghurt		65	95	130	160	195	225	255
Juices, Sour Cream		65	95	130	160	195	225	255

Use as required to assist in estimating recipe weight

Table 3

Volume conversions to nearest logical amount

Fluid oz.	Pint	Millilitre	Litre	Teaspoon	Metric Tablespoon	Cup	Australian Tablespoon
		5		1			
		10		2			
		15		3	1	1/16	
		20		4			1
1		25		5			
	1/16	30			2	1/8	
		40		8			2
		45		9	3		
2		50		10			
	1/8	60		12	4	¼	3
3		75			5		
		80		16			4
		85				1/3*	
	3/16	90			6	3/8	
4		100		20			5

Fluid oz.	Pint	Millilitre	Litre	Teaspoon	Metric Tablespoon	Cup	Australian Tablespoon
5	¼	125	⅛		8	½	6
6		150					
		155			10	⅝	
		170			11	⅔**	
	⅜	185			12	¾	
8		200		40	13		10
		220			14	⅞	
10	½	250	¼		16	1	12
		280			18	1⅛	
12		300		60			15
	⅝	310			20	1¼	
14		350					
15	¾	375	⅜		24	1½	
	⅞	440			28	1¾	
20	1	500	½		32	2	25
30	1½	750	¾		48	3	
40	2	1,000	1			4	50
60	2½	1,500	1½			6	

* Equals 3/8 cup less 1 teaspoon

** Equals 5/8 cup plus 1 tablespoon

help !

Call for Help !

Are you having problems with your machine malfunctioning and don't know where to go for parts or service in your area?
Or, are you having trouble finding a supplier of certain ingredients?
Or you just can't get the right result from a recipe you want to impress everybody with?

Call for Help !

Do you want to buy international metric cup and spoon measures?
Or oven gloves and don't know where to get them?

Call for Help !

Telephone (or fax) the 'Daley Bread' message centre at Wellington on (04) 589-4094 and listen to the instructions.
Or write to 'Daley Bread' PO Box 38020, Wellington Mail Centre.

Advice is free. You pay only for your phone call, postage or fax to me.
Remember to ask for my mail order list of ingredients and other essential accessories - all tested, all recommended by 'Daley Bread'.

Whether you phone, write or fax, remember to give your name, address and phone or fax number, and the details of your machine.

If you have a breadmaker experience to relate, or an original recipe you would like to pass on, please contact me as above. (A letter is best. It costs less and can be as long as you like.)

Happy breadmaking !

George Dale

Daley Bread
TM

index